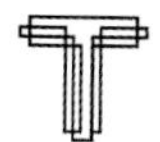

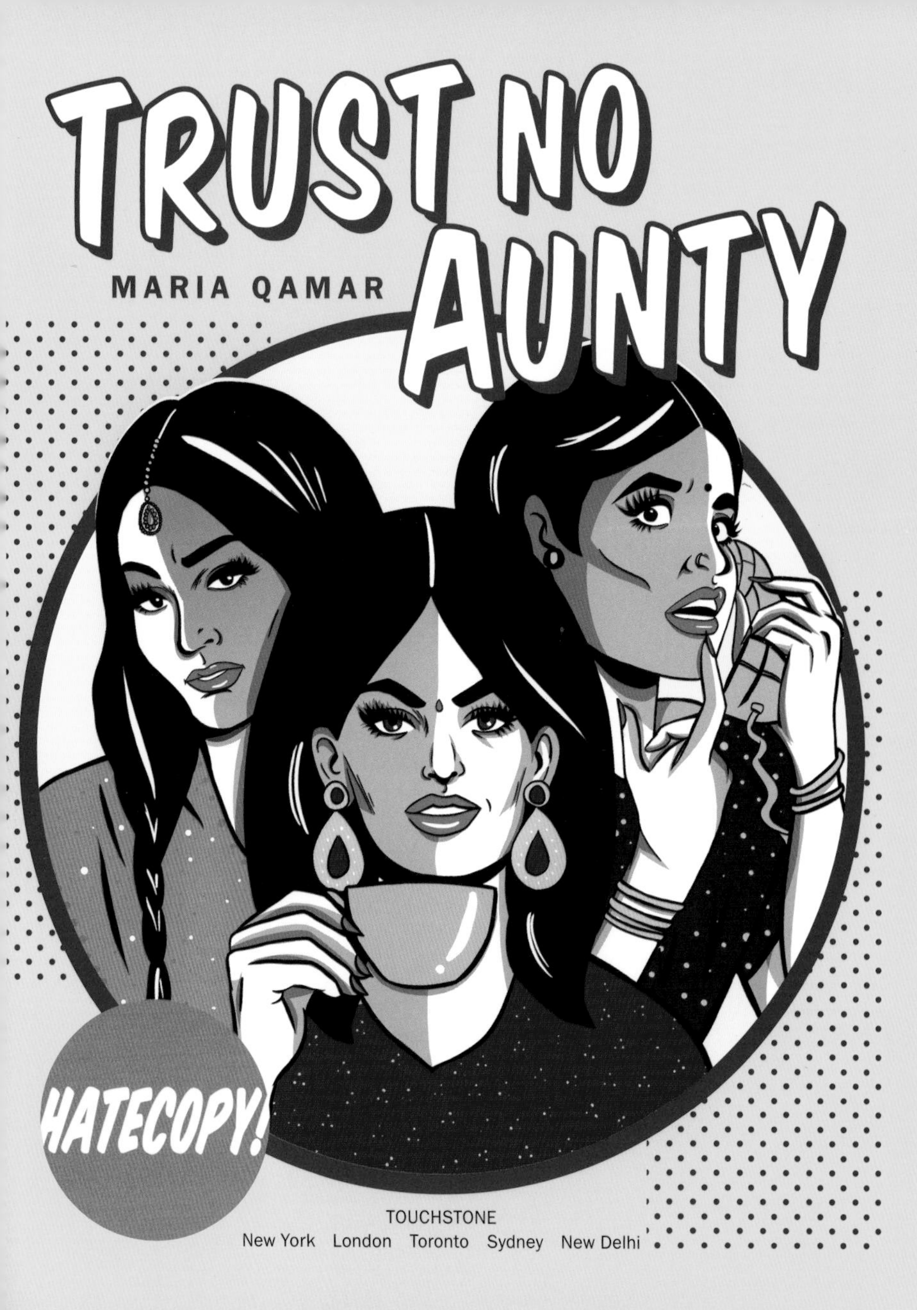
TRUST NO AUNTY
MARIA QAMAR
HATECOPY!
TOUCHSTONE
New York London Toronto Sydney New Delhi

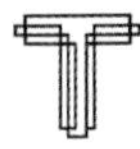

TOUCHSTONE
An Imprint of Simon & Schuster, Inc.
1230 Avenue of the Americas
New York, NY 10020

First Touchstone hardcover edition August 2017

TOUCHSTONE and colophon are registered trademarks of Simon & Schuster, Inc.

For information about special discounts for bulk purchases, please contact Simon & Schuster Special Sales at 1-866-506-1949 or business@simonandschuster.com.

The Simon & Schuster Speakers Bureau can bring authors to your live event. For more information or to book an event, contact the Simon & Schuster Speakers Bureau at 866-248-3049 or visit our website at www.simonspeakers.com.

Interior design by Richard Dao

Manufactured in the United States of America

10 9 8 7 6 5 4 3 2 1

Library of Congress Cataloging-in-Publication Data

Names: Qamar, Maria, author. | Instagram (Firm)
Title: Trust no aunty / Maria Qamar.
Description: First Touchstone hardcover edition | New York : Touchstone, 2017. | Description based on print version record and CIP data provided by publisher; resource not viewed.
Identifiers: LCCN 2016055717 (print) | LCCN 2017011766 (ebook) | ISBN 9781501154744 (Ebook) | ISBN 9781501154737 (hardback)
Subjects: LCSH: Family—Humor. | Aunts—Humor. | BISAC: HUMOR / Topic / Relationships. | HUMOR / Topic / Marriage & Family.
Classification: LCC PN6231.F3 (ebook) | LCC PN6231.F3 Q36 2017 (print) | DDC 305.8/914071—dc23
LC record available at https://lccn.loc.gov/2016055717

ISBN 978-1-5011-5473-7
ISBN 978-1-5011-5474-4 (ebook)

THIS BOOK IS DEDICATED TO MY AUNTIES,
YOUR AUNTIES, AND THE AUNTY
WE WILL ALL EVENTUALLY BECOME

YOU CANNOT GIVE ME ANY ADVICE!

—Kanye West

CONTENTS

PART 4. BEAUTY, BODY, AND COLOR

PART 5. DOMESTIC SKILLS THAT PAY THE BILLS

THERE'S NO SUCH THING AS TOO MUCH GUPSHUP!!

PART 6. LIFE, STYLE, AND LIFESTYLE

TRUST NO AUNTY

BESHARAM! HOW COULD YOU?!

AUNTY

NOUN | AUNT•IE | \ 'AN-TĒ, 'ÄN-\

Aunty is a term of endearment (and sometimes insult) used to describe an older woman. The aunty is a cross-cultural phenomenon that isn't limited to a family member; she could be a neighbor, a family friend, or just some lady on the bus who wants to throw some casual black magic your way. Most commonly featured in Indian soap operas, an aunty is a feisty and dramatic powerhouse of a woman who enters your house with plans to take over your life for a very small and strangely particular reason. When aunties combine into groups of two or more, their plotting power is instantly multiplied. They are at family parties or friendly get-togethers with your mother, finding ways to make your life difficult, trying to get you married to their sons, and telling you to lose weight while simultaneously trying to feed you a second dinner.

As an aunty-survivor and a woman who has lived the cross-cultural experience, I am here to remind you: Trust no aunty. We've all experienced "aunty interference" that has hindered our social growth and embarrassed us in front of our friends and cool cousins. I've defied the advice of my aunties almost every step of the way, and I've turned out fine—fantastic, even. Until I started putting my art about the South Asian–American experience into the world, I didn't know just how many others had gone through the same confusing culture clash while trying to find their way. If you thought you were alone in dealing with the overwhelming, meddling, yet oddly comforting attention of the aunties in your life, I've written this book for you.

INTRODUCTION

HOLD UP! WAIT A MINUTE! WHAT DO YOU THINK YOU'RE DOING????? SHOULDN'T YOU BE STUDYING? OR LEARNING HOW TO ROLL THE ROUNDEST POSSIBLE ROTI? OR PRAYING FOR FORGIVENESS FOR ALL THE DIRTY, DIRTY THINGS YOU DID LAST WEEKEND?! LISTEN, KID, YOU CAN'T BE POLLUTING YOUR MIND WITH BOOKS LIKE THESE; YOU'VE GOT TO MAKE SPACE FOR ALL THE CHAPTERS IN YOUR TEXTBOOKS. THOSE PARABOLAS WON'T . . . UH . . . BEND THEMSELVES!

Just kidding. But not really. These are the kind of things you would expect me to say if I was your aunty. Lucky for you, I am not. In these pages, I will be the best friend who annoys the hell out of you but also doesn't tell your parents about the liquor you stole from their cabinet that night we got trashed while watching *Mean Girls* in the basement. I will teach you how to deal with nosy aunties, make bomb food for, like, ten dollars, go on dates without getting caught by overprotective parents, and other cool things you can do with your other friends when you inevitably put this book down and ditch me tomorrow.

I was born in a home which was half Gujarati and half Bihari, by way of Bangladesh but located in Pakistan, so I was raised with four different cultures that seemed to be in conflict all the freakin' time. When I moved to the middle-class suburbs in a cold, cold land called Canada in the year 2000, we adopted a fifth culture.

I always got picked on for being too brown or not brown enough at home and outside of it, until I finally snapped and said, "YOU KNOW WHAT, GUYS, I'M SORRY, BUT I GOTTA GO TAKE A WALK TO THE ART SUPPLY STORE AND

DRAW EVERYTHING SO I CAN FIGURE OUT WHAT YOU GUYS ARE SO MAD AT ME FOR. BRB."

And draw I did. I drew and drew until I found you. I juggled two identities: a traditional desi (a person of Indian, Pakistani, or Bangladeshi birth who lives abroad) and a Western punk. Against all odds, I became a strong, independent, and sometimes mouthy person who loves both of these identities. I believe in being honest about who you are and embracing it, flaws and all. It's the first step towards attaining the freedom to do whatever the hell you want despite the obstacles and judgment that might come with doing those things. And preparing yourself for judgment is one of the most important things you can do. This is why I say, Trust no aunty.

Growing up in the West, I gravitated towards aunties because they were the ones who delivered weird and wonderful wisdom about hair health and long-term relationships, and sometimes straight-up-enraging reminders of the flawed traditions favoring our uncles, like women compromising education for marriage. We're constantly told to eat more and weigh less, become doctors/ lawyers/engineers but also have three children by twenty-three, study hard but also cook up a storm. As the advice becomes more and more contradictory and the world shifts further and further away from traditional practices, you might realize that the person you need to trust most is yourself. And me, of course.

PART 1
IN SC

HOOL

SPICE METER

3 out of 10 green chilies. Not dangerous, and is probably good to have around if only to keep you from taking that fourth shot of gin at frosh orientation.

CHARACTERISTICS

Aunties aren't born aunties. First, they are molded by their predecessors and trained rigorously in the arts of plotting, black magic, and neighborhood gossip. These are the aunties in training (AITs). They may look young, but they possess the wisdom of a household of veteran aunties poking their eyes, ears, and rolling pins around every corner.

WHERE YOU MIGHT FIND THEM

The AIT is often found in our very own social circles, offering relationship advice that always begins with "He's nice but . . ." and ends with "I think you should end it."

STRENGTHS

The AIT is on a mission to create the perfect world full of perfect girls—but none more perfect than her. She has mastered the art of the passive-aggressive "told you so" when you need it the least. And somehow, between exams, relationships, social outings, and professional life, the AIT has perfected her culinary skills and is always there to help heal, feed, and bring you back to life after you've broken up with Chad for the fifth time.

WEAKNESSES

Since the AIT is only a trainee, she is bound to possess certain weaknesses her mentors do not, such as occasionally saying something genuinely helpful and keeping your white boyfriend Brad a secret. Warning: This does not mean you are safe from judgment.

SCENARIO 1

YOU ARE OUT IN THE AFTERNOON. AN AIT WILL REMIND YOU OF YOUR CURFEW EVERY HOUR ON THE HOUR BUT WILL STAY UNTIL THE VERY END, JUST SO SHE CAN CONTINUE TO REMIND YOU ON THE WAY BACK. THIS WILL MAKE YOU FEEL LIKE THE DISAPPOINTMENT YOU WILL UNDOUBTEDLY BE TO YOUR POOR, POOR FAMILY.

ROOKIE MOVE

Give in and go home early. Eat some daal chawal. Watch *American Idol* reruns. Go to bed at seven. Get married at twenty-three. Have two children. Work in accounting. Die slowly.

BOSS MOVE

Remind her of the curfew we all have—the curfew called life. The clock stops for no one, so we might as well make the most of the time we have before it's all over. Plus, the club doesn't open until ten. What would you rather do? Sneak out later? ***THAT'S WAY WORSE.***

PITAJI WOULD KILL US IF HE FOUND OUT...
PITAJI DON'T KNOW SHIT, SHRUTI...

SCENARIO II

PROM IS COMING UP. SHAD HAS ASKED YOU OUT. YOU ARE NOT ALLOWED TO DANCE WITH BOYS BEFORE MARRIAGE. THE AIT DISAPPROVES BECAUSE SHE KNOWS THE TROUBLE YOU WILL BE IN IF PITAJI (DEAR OLD DAD) FINDS OUT ON SOCIAL MEDIA THE MORNING AFTER.

ROOKIE MOVE

Listen to her and go to the prom solo. No one wants to wake up to the chappal.*

BOSS MOVE

Go with Shad. Fall in love. Continue dating through college. Have beautiful babies and put them in a talent show. The next Zayn Malik is born. You've won at life.

*Slipper. You will get hit with a slipper.

WHY AREN'T YOU MARRIED YET?!!
I'M ONLY 12, MOM, WTF...

SCENARIO III

YOU HAVE INVITED YOUR AIT OVER TO SHOW YOUR PARENTS THAT NOT ALL OF YOUR FRIENDS ARE SCUMBAGS. THEY NOW LOVE HER MORE THAN YOU.

Never bring her around again because they will keep comparing you to her for the rest of your life.

Bring her around more so your family believes her best behavior is rubbing off on you. You are now an angel (and future aunty) by association.

BE MORE LIKE SARAH! SHE HAS A NICE FACE!

WHAT YOUR MOTHER THINKS YOU'RE UP TO WHEN YOU'RE OUT
OUR DAUGHTER DIDN'T PICK UP THE PHONE, VINAY! SHE'S OBVIOUSLY DEAD!!!

7:00A.M.

"She is working. She will make us proud. She is a good beti (daughter) who will get married tomorrow and make us all so very, very happy. Bless her soul."

12:00P.M.

"She is a good girl who attends the library at appropriate hours and definitely does not hang out with the opposite sex for whatever reason."

3:00P.M.

"IT IS GETTING LATE. MUST CALL HER TWENTY TIMES TO MAKE SURE SHE IS ON HER WAY HOME."

3:30P.M.

"SHE DID NOT PICK UP HER PHONE. SHE IS DEAD."

6:00P.M.

"SHE IS DEAD. MUST CALL POLICE."

7:00P.M.

"MUST VISIT PRINTING SHOP TO MAKE SURE HER FACE IS PLASTERED ALL OVER THE CITY BECAUSE SHE IS NOT PICKING UP HER PHONE AND SHE IS DEFINITELY DEAD."

7:05P.M.

"SHE HAS CALLED US BACK AND SAYS SHE IS STILL AT THE LIBRARY WITH PREETI. WE WILL CONTINUE TO PANIC UNTIL SHE IS HOME."

9:00P.M.

"THE SPAWN OF SATAN HAS CURSED OUR HOME AND IS NOW OUT TO DESTROY OUR FAMILY VALUES THROUGH THIS VESSEL WE CALL A DAUGHTER. WE MUST INVITE THE EXTENDED FAMILY OVER TO PRAY FOR FORGIVENESS."

11:00P.M.

"PRAYING CIRCLE BEGINS. OUR COUSINS IN INDIA, KENYA, AND ZIMBABWE HAVE JOINED US THROUGH SKYPE. WE ARE HOLDING HANDS AND CHANTING TOGETHER."

12:00A.M.

"LET'S GET THE SLIPPERS, BELTS, AND LADLES READY FOR HER ARRIVAL, FOR SHE IS ABSOLUTELY AND ROYALLY FUCKED."

TOP FIVE AMERICAN HIGH SCHOOL EXPERIENCES THAT WILL TRAUMATIZE A DESI TEEN

The hours between 8:30 A.M. and 3:30 P.M. were part of my daily escape from the drama in my house. I got to talk about boys, gossip about the girls, rant about the arts, roast my teachers, and generally discuss subjects I couldn't with my family. But it wasn't until I moved on to my adult life that I realized how much I craved the day-to-day theatrics of being a troubled teen; and it felt exactly like a soap opera I loved to watch.

CRUSHING ON A BOY OF A DIFFERENT RACE

This is a no-brainer. After the constant pressure you start to receive from your family about marrying a nice Indian boy, you decided to fall in love with Matthew. He's tall, Italian, athletic, and funny and also Italian. Did I mention he's Italian? Do you introduce koftas as meatballs? Do you pretend that his total family gathering is only one-tenth of your immediate family gathering? Do you let him believe that you'd rather watch *Iron Man* than the new Shah Rukh Khan flick? Does Matthew know your mother won't let you out past sunset? DOES MATTHEW KNOW YOU DO NOT ACTUALLY STORE YOGURT IN THAT CONTAINER?

GETTING CAUGHT DRINKING AT A BASEMENT PARTY

Damn, you finally got invited to the Friday-night basement/garage sesh at the house of the cool Punjabi kid with the chill parents who travel often. You have also been tasked with bringing the liquor because, unfortunately for you, you're just a little taller and hairier than the rest of the crew. This means you can pass for an older sibling, and older siblings always help out. But you're also a swagless idiot who has never done this before, so you end up using the credit card your parents lent you for emergencies, the statement of which is delivered directly to them at your home address. The ass-whooping to follow is colossal, but so is the respect earned by taking one for the team. Kudos.

PICKING A HALLOWEEN OUTFIT

You decided to be a ballerina and your very Ukrainian best friend Katya decided to be an INDIAN PRINCESS. Now, you and Katya are totes chill: you walk to school together, you swap some of her pierogies for your kebabs at lunch, you have a handful of inside jokes about the new substitute teacher, and sometimes you even end up wearing the same outfit. But this little incident was something you saw coming. You probably even spent the last few weeks hoping and praying that this wouldn't happen. Having a problematic friend is a nightmare because explaining to someone how they are being racist rarely ends with a thank-you and a warm embrace. Better find a new source of pierogies, because Princess Katya's getting cut.

JOINING A SPORTS TEAM AND ACTUALLY BEING GOOD

You could be the best damn soccer player in the world and an aunty will always remind you that boys will never go for a girl with such muscular calves. You gotta block and dodge that criticism like you do the punches in your tae kwon do classes. You gotta sprint 5K away from the sneers and commentary. You gotta dunk on the haters 24/7. I don't know any more sports references, but you get my point. Tell Auntyji to HUT HUT!*

TAKING AN ART CLASS

Oh, you've crossed the line now. Painting? Interpretive dancing? NUDE DRAWING CLASSES? You might as well have taken Slipper Whipping 101 so you can learn all the ways you'll get your ass beat for trying to become anything other than a doctor. It's cool though, because in order to become a successful artist you've got to be a little bit messed up in the head. This is exactly what your family will help with when you inform them about your new pursuit. It's bittersweet absorbing all that shame and disappointment while knowing you're going to channel it into great art. Thanks, Auntyji!

*GTFO

RECIPES FOR THE DESI CAMPUS GIRL ON A BUDGET

There are a lot of good things about moving out of Mummy and Papa's house. You can take hour-long baths, wear your miniskirt without having to throw sweatpants over it, and finally get PHYSICAL—if you know what I mean.

But one thing that you will miss and might not be able to live without is Mom's cooking. Despite the perks of living alone and finally being independent, the smell of tharka and fifteen different spices all circulating in the house 24/7 just won't be around to keep you guessing what's for dinner. Don't worry, Author Aunty (that's me!) is here to help.

During my college days, my roommates sustained and suppressed their hunger by mixing canned beans and canned tuna in a large bowl, eating it unheated and uncooked. I, on the other hand, spent way too much money on ramen and precooked, prepackaged junk. Eventually my stomach began to turn at the thought of eating 1,200 milligrams of sodium for dinner and I began to look for cheaper alternatives to eating on campus. And who better to seek advice from on saving money than my Gujju mom, who on a small entry-level salary managed to feed (and sometimes overfeed) a family of four every night for DECADES!

This is when I learned the magic of the desi staple: daal chawal, otherwise known as lentils and rice. Daal is the kind of dish that can be made as a side or a hearty main depending on your mood. I normally made my daal thick because my mood was usually "too broke to buy meat." Plus, lentils are a good source of potassium, calcium, zinc, niacin, and vitamin K, AND are hella rich in dietary fiber, lean protein, folate, and iron. You are going to be so fit you'll start endorsing teatoxes and waist trainers on your social media in no time. To this day, I use my college daal recipe to impress the hell out of everybody, including my mom.

SHE STOLE
MY HUSBAND
BUT SHE CAN
NEVER STEAL
THIS RECIPE!

BEST DAAL EVER

WHAT YOU'LL NEED

Oil *($10? I don't know. I just borrow it from roommates or my mom.)*
Ginger garlic paste *(borrow some from your mom, or grab one from the store for $2)*
Turmeric *($1)*
Cumin *($1)*
Coriander *($1)*
Chili powder *($1)*
Black pepper
Salt
Green chili *($1–$2)*
Onions *($2–$3 per three-pound bag)*
Tomatoes *(optional)*
Red split lentils *($3–$5)*
Fresh cilantro
Basmati rice *($11 for literally one of those insanely heavy thousand-pound body bags of rice that will last for two generations after you. Or just borrow some from your mom.)*

HOW TO MAKE IT

Get off the phone with the pizza guy and walk to the kitchen. Honestly, you're starving, and the fastest way to eat is to start cooking and taste as you go.

You there yet? Okay, good. Take out a pot and pour some oil into it. Put the pot on a burner and turn the flame to medium-high. Wait for the oil to get hot (you'll know it's hot when you see little bubbles at the bottom).

Cool. Add two heaping tablespoons of ginger garlic paste. You can add one if you're scared. Now, stand back because this will splatter. Turn the heat down when that happens, for obvious reasons.

Add in all the spices with a TEASPOON. NOT A TABLESPOON. Add turmeric, cumin, coriander, chili powder, black pepper, and salt. Also break a green chili in half and throw that bad boy in there. If you have other spices you wanna add, now is the time.

Dice up half an onion or a whole one (depending on how much you like onions) and throw them in the pot. Mix the onions with the spices.

Take a deep whiff. It should smell like your parents' house. You can add tomatoes and keep frying if you want. It's optional.

Now that you've transformed into an aunty, turn down the heat to low and step away from the pot to take out your lentils.

Rinse the lentils in a strainer or a bowl until the water is somewhat clear. Then put the lentils in the pot. Turn the heat up to medium or high and mix it all together.

You are ALMOST DONE. OMG, ISN'T THAT EXCITING? Okay. Now add enough water to the pot so it's, like, just a little above the lentils. Throw in a huge handful of fresh cilantro, mix in, and cover with a lid.

Keep checking, like, every five minutes to make sure nothing is stuck to the bottom and to see if the daal has softened up. If your water is evaporating and your daal still isn't melty and soft, you can keep adding water little by little until it is. If you're brown, chances are you've had daal before, so just do this until you are SURE that your daal looks and tastes like the daal you've had before. I let my daal cook for about 15 to 20 minutes on medium high and add a lot of cumin and cilantro at the end.

Now that you're waiting for your LENTIL CURRY (aka daal) to be nice and soft, you can put 1 cup of rice in a rice cooker or a pot with 2 cups water and cook that so the two can be done at the same time. The rice should take no more than 15 minutes to cook.

THAT'S IT! And the best part about this recipe is that with the ingredients you've bought for less than $15, you can keep making this delicious recipe over and over for literally weeks. If you have extra cash you can sauté some ground beef to put on top of the daal. Good luck, beti! I'm rooting for you!

As desis, we spend so much of our eating time feeling guilty because everything in our cuisine is based on carbs and a colossal amount of ghee. And when it comes to desserts, the situation is even worse. For example, kheer is a popular dessert made with RICE and MILK mixed with a shit ton of SUGAR and BUTTER and consumed by the bowlful. It's served on every special occasion, mastered by every aunty, and cannot be turned down. It's also a little hard to acquire when you live miles away from your parents. But what if I told you that you could have kheer whenever you wanted and be in the best shape of your life? Lucky for us, because I stumbled upon the greatest health hack of our lifetime, that's exactly what I am telling you.

KHEER ZARA

WHAT YOU'LL NEED

Chia seeds *($7–$11 per bag. I KNOW, I KNOW, JUST TRUST ME.)*
Coconut milk *($2–$3 for a can or carton)*
Cardamom powder *(or seeds) ($1)*
Sugar *($1)*
Saffron *(if you're fancy) (I have never bought saffron. Just get some from your mom.)*

HOW TO MAKE IT

Okay, now that you've shopped like a white girl who just learned the meaning of namaste, you're ready to make some KHEER!

Take two TABLESPOONS of chia seeds and put them into a medium-sized microwave-safe bowl.

Take two TABLESPOONS of coconut milk and add it to the bowl.

Take a pinch of cardamom powder or seeds and add it to the bowl.

Take about two TEASPOONS (or tablespoons, depending on how sweet you'd like your kheer) of sugar and add it to the bowl.

You can add saffron now if you'd like, but I'm too cheap for that.

Now, DON'T MIX IT. DON'T TOUCH IT. Put the bowl into the microwave for only 10 to 15 SECONDS (until the coconut milk becomes liquid).

Remove the bowl from the microwave and stir everything together until the chia seeds begin to expand and become soft. Let the bowl sit for 30 seconds.

Your CHIA KHEER is ready! I ate this for breakfast for about two weeks and dropped five pounds; it was insane. And it tastes exactly like kheer without the long cooking process and carbs. TRY IT NOW, YOU LAZY BUM.

HOW TO STAY FOCUSED IN SCHOOL WHEN ALL OF YOUR FRIENDS ARE GETTING MARRIED

This may seem counterintuitive, but when I turned fifteen, my parents began pressuring me about marriage as a way to keep me from having a boyfriend. You see, I wasn't allowed to have a boyfriend so if I was talking to a boy, my parents made it known that I better be planning to marry him. This tactic was oddly effective.

In our culture we talk about marriage before we talk about sex, love, or even our periods (if we even talk about those things). I once knew a girl in the eleventh grade who was arranged to be married to a boy but had no idea what she had to do on her wedding night; she didn't even know what her vagina was or how it worked. And when you're SURROUNDED by girls constantly chatting about the lifelong commitment that is marriage before they even start college, it's a little hard to focus on the goals you've set for yourself that don't involve Ajay and your 2.5 kids. Here's how you can stay on top of your studies while everyone in the world around you is getting hitched.

Stay friends with single people. It sounds harsh, but avoiding those who consistently yap about flowers and sarees and table settings during exam week will help keep you sane. When you need a break from the books, chat with the few friends you have that don't plan on getting married anytime soon.

Be decisive. If you're going to do something, do it all the way. If you're applying for grad school, but are worried about not having a child until you're thirty, just do it anyway. Sacrificing your dreams for the sake of marriage or children is a ploy by the aunties to keep you chained to the patriarchy. FIGHT THE POWER. APPLY NOW.

Amplify your personal accomplishments. Every time the word marriage is mentioned in conversation with your family, mention your accomplishments in school. Mention a new job you're applying for or how amazing your next project is going to be. Drive home the fact that you are and will continue to be more than just a bride. Make your worth known every chance you get.

Visit more libraries and less fam jams. It's okay to miss a family party if it means that you'll get a few more hours to study. You don't need to attend all ten days of a wedding or the prewedding parties. Skipping your exam prep to spend an entire day with aunties who try to set you up with Bunty and Chintu next door isn't the least bit productive. Stay away when you can.

Avoid Bollywood at all costs. The last thing you need before an important deadline is the urge to drop it all and go dance in a field with your boyfriend. While B-wood is amazing for getting you through breakups or an eleven-hour flight to India, it's absolutely deadly during studies. Almost all good Bollywood films are based on the idea of romance and marriage, and more often than not have a poor damsel in distress plot line that will have you wishing that a man more successful and educated than you would come save you from writing tomorrow's paper. This will not happen. Be your own hero. Save your damn self. Search for love over spring break or something.

In the end, just remember, wedding SZN will pass and you WILL survive. Enjoy yourself, eat lots, and support your girlfriends and/or guy friends through their special day, but if it's too soon for you to consider it for yourself (and trust yourself, you'll know if it's too soon), don't worry. There is absolutely nothing wrong with going against the matrimonial grain. **AUTHOR AUNTY'S GOT YOUR BACK.**

PRO-
FES
MAKE SOMETHING OF YOUR LIFE ALREADY!

PART 2
IONAL
LIFE

SPICE METER

8 out of 10 green chilies. Pretty spicy with the insults. You are broke. She is not. This is and forever will be the nature of your relationship and the subtext of all conversation for the rest of your lives.

CHARACTERISTICS

Behind every uncle is a CEO aunty, holding their Black Card and simultaneously yelling at him for his incompetence. Her marriage was an arrangement between two wealthy empires to build a bigger empire to take over America one mechanically processed roti at a time. She is fierce, has an MBBS, can speak five different languages, and can cook up a storm while on a conference call. She has three spoiled college dropouts who won't stop mooching off the bank of Mummy and Papa.

WHERE YOU MIGHT FIND THEM

CEO aunties are always the last to show up to a family dinner, just so the entire khandan* can watch them roll up in the new Lexus.

STRENGTHS

CEO aunty is good at sharing the wealth (even if it's only to remind you that she has it), so when you need a little extra cash to take Preeti out to dinner, she'll probably give you a summer gig in the family business. Don't expect to be paid a lot, though. This is after all a FAMILY business. You're lucky to be getting paid at all.

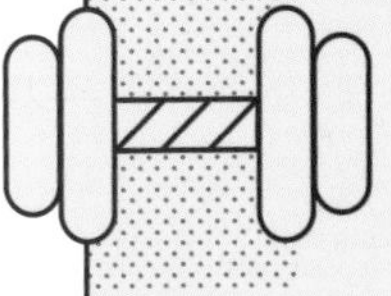

WEAKNESSES

The only thing Auntyji loves more than Uncle's Amex is her ladla† son named some variation of Ricky or Vicky. Try not to break his heart.

*Extended and immediate family; anyone and everyone you're related to or talked to.

†Mama's boy.

SCENARIO 1

YOU HAVE ENTERED CEO AUNTY'S HOME FOR A DAWAT* OF SORTS. SHE ASKS WHAT YOU DO FOR A LIVING—AND YOU KNOW SHE'S ASKING ONLY BECAUSE SHE WANTS TO TALK SMACK ABOUT YOUR LIFE CHOICES.

ROOKIE MOVE

Tell her the truth and then slowly feel the heat of judgment engulf you like Mumbai heat.

BOSS MOVE

Tell her you have exactly one PhD in minding your own business. Write her a recommendation.

*A lunch/dinner party held for families, both related and unrelated.

I WOULD MIND MY OWN BUSINESS IF I HAD ANY...

SCENARIO II

CEO AUNTY KEEPS CALLING YOU OUT DURING MEETINGS AND TRIES TO BABY YOU IN THE WORKPLACE.

Tell her that you are your own person and that her behavior is extremely unprofessional.

Be the biggest baby you can be until she eventually sees you as part of the family. Bring her homemade paranthas, ask for advice in personal matters, rub her feet—whatever you think will get you in so you can get mad promotions and take over the family business.

BETA, YOU'RE ALWAYS ON THE PHONE!
I'M A FUCKING RECEPTIONIST!

SCENARIO III

CEO AUNTY HAS DECIDED TO TAKE YOU OFF A PROJECT BECAUSE YOU SEEM TO BE WORKING TOO CLOSELY WITH HER HUSBAND.

Take the L and move on to whatever task is assigned next. She probably has the right to be suspicious and you should respect her wishes.

Tell her that you were just keeping an eye on him because you saw him consistently flirting with Parvati in accounting. Bond with CEO aunty. Finesse a raise.

SORRY I'M LATE. I HAD A LOT OF PAPERWORK AT THE OFFICE...
PAPERWORK... OR PARVATI?!

SCENARIO IV

CEO AUNTY IS NOW SHARING PERSONAL STORIES OF YOU WHEN YOU WERE A BABY WITH YOUR COWORKERS.

ROOKIE MOVE

Laugh nervously while inching towards the paper towels to cover up your profuse sweating. Look on LinkedIn for a new job the next day.

BOSS MOVE

Ask her how old she is now.
WARNING: You will get slapped.

YOU BADTAMEEZ BITCH!

So you don't want to be a doctor, lawyer, engineer, or accountant. I guess your life's over.

JUST KIDDING. This is where things get SPICY! With the right attitude, choosing an unconventional career is exciting and extremely beneficial not just to you but to everyone around you as well.

If you can't decide which career you wish to pursue but know that Cubicle City isn't right for you, consult this little chart.

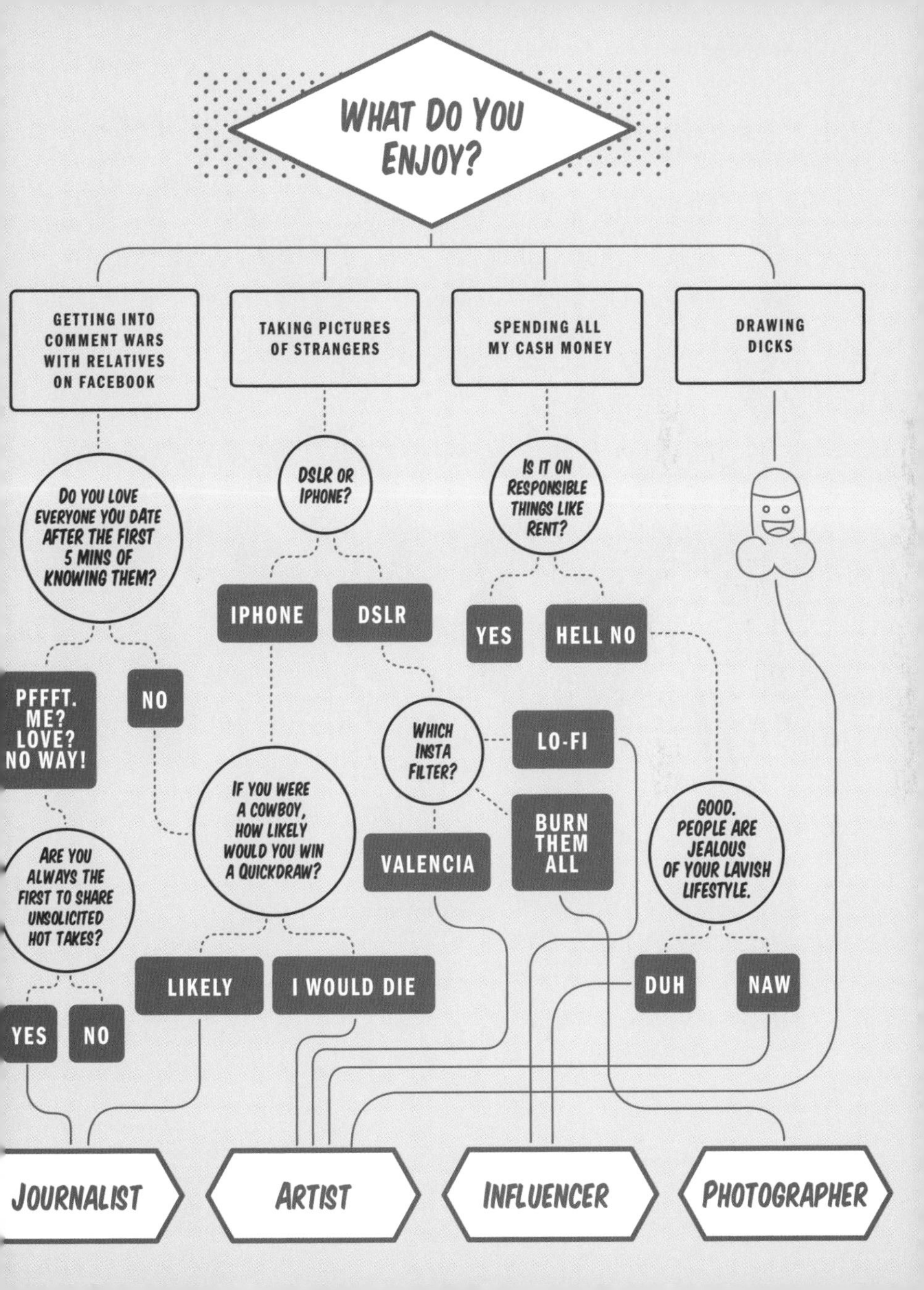

WHAT DO YOU ENJOY?
GETTING INTO COMMENT WARS WITH RELATIVES ON FACEBOOK
TAKING PICTURES OF STRANGERS
SPENDING ALL MY CASH MONEY
DRAWING DICKS
DO YOU LOVE EVERYONE YOU DATE AFTER THE FIRST 5 MINS OF KNOWING THEM?
DSLR OR IPHONE?
IS IT ON RESPONSIBLE THINGS LIKE RENT?
IPHONE
DSLR
YES
HELL NO
PFFFT. ME? LOVE? NO WAY!
NO
WHICH INSTA FILTER?
LO-FI
BURN THEM ALL
VALENCIA
IF YOU WERE A COWBOY, HOW LIKELY WOULD YOU WIN A QUICKDRAW?
GOOD. PEOPLE ARE JEALOUS OF YOUR LAVISH LIFESTYLE.
ARE YOU ALWAYS THE FIRST TO SHARE UNSOLICITED HOT TAKES?
LIKELY
I WOULD DIE
DUH
NAW
YES
NO
JOURNALIST
ARTIST
INFLUENCER
PHOTOGRAPHER

EXPLAINING A CAREER

Okay, now that you've chosen an unconventional career, it's time for the hardest part: explaining it to Mom and Dad.

Blogger (including vloggers): If you are a first-generation desi like me, chances are Mum and Dad won't understand what this word means. AT ALL. Be sure to use terms like *long-form journalism* and *thinkpiece*, as well as *brand sponsorships* and *grassroots marketing*. These things are somewhat related to blogging but, more than that, are buzzy and important-sounding enough to keep the questions to a minimum. But never forget that blogging *is* a business, one that requires balancing creativity and marketing savvy to write and to push content to thousands, sometimes millions of viewers around the world!

Art director: When I worked in advertising, I used to get partnered up with art directors to come up with cool campaigns for big brands. Did you see the crazy ad where Red Bull made a dude jump out of a spaceship onto the earth? Or the Old Spice Guy?! I didn't write those. But I know who did! The art director's job is to make things look flawless on paper and on-screen. To explain this to your family you should again use words like *marketing* and *campaigns* and phrases like "handling large budgets" and "directing brand aesthetics." I don't know exactly what that last one means, but it sounds hella important.

Lifestyle influencer: Oh, man, this one is TOUGH. You have chosen to adopt the Kardashian lifestyle, and now you have to explain to your very private and protective father that you will be snapping photos and endorsing hair gummies during Christmas. Using words like *brand ambassador* and *marketing influencer* will help to give them a gist of what your day-to-day is like, how you are "the catalyst for driving a niche market for specific brands." And the best part is, you can do it all from the comfort of your Pinterest-perfect home office.

Artist: One of my biggest challenges was explaining to my desi family that I had decided to be broke and sleepless for two consecutive years. Depending on whether you pursue fine arts, writing, animation, or graphic design, there are various buzzwords you can use to sway your family into thinking you're on the right "path." Phrases like "government-approved grants," "global residencies," and "building partnerships with private galleries and businesses to drive profit" will ease the mind of a panicking mother who fears that you are trading in your rotis for canvas.

Freelancer: You don't like working for someone else (and maybe you don't like working) AND THAT IS OKAY! Of all careers, this one is my personal fave because you're taking control of just how much time you spend working for someone else. You also get some much-deserved "you time" when you need it, while still making (hopefully) a comfortable living. If you are a single parent or a new mommy, or just want to travel every other month and don't want to sit at a desk all day, this is perfect for you. Explain to Mummyji and Papaji that freelancing is essentially "working from home." You deal with the same day-to-day tasks as someone in an office but on a project-by-project, client-by-client basis. Using phrases like "scope creep" and "client pitch" helps to spruce up the definition a little bit. Just don't let them know you actually spend 99 percent of your day watching videos of happy corgis on Instagram.

HOW I STOPPED WORKING AND ENJOYED MY ZINDAGI

If I were to go back in time and act as an older didi* to myself when I was a nineteen-year-old, full of potential and Red Bull, I'd tell me to "Stop working so hard, beti." There is a lot of pressure on young people, particularly in our community, to begin working as soon and as hard as possible. A strong work ethic and nonstop hustle are classic immigrant virtues and I was taught to value stability above all else. But WTF does *stability* even mean for someone who barely got the chance to experience the rockiness of real life? How could my family expect me to "settle down" when I'd never gotten the chance to stand up on my own two feet? Damn, I should be a songwriter.

I heard my parents talk about this abstract idea of stability and it was always linked to the promise of my own family and a steady paycheck. I was constantly in a state of panic, stuck in the cycle of "what-ifs?" "What if I never get the job?" "What if I never work at a desk?" "What if I never get paid to do things because of that one time I got kicked out of class for putting on lipstick during a lecture?" Eventually, I learned that my mental and emotional stability should come first. Here are the steps I took to find that balance.

I LEFT WORK AT 5 P.M. ONCE

There are few things worse than clocking in at 9 A.M. Monday morning to a job you don't like. Clocking out at midnight was one of them. I always assumed that I had to work until everyone in the building left or else I'd get fired and get flamed on LinkedIn for being a lazy idiot. But one day I

*Older sister or cousin.

sneaked out of work at regular adult hours and discovered that there were so many activities I could do before passing out from exhaustion and waking up in a pool of my own drool at 7 A.M. the next day. I discovered Netflix. I discovered I could afford Netflix. I discovered I could drink wine while watching Netflix, etc.

I SPENT TIME WITH MY MOM

I suffer from FOMO. A lot. Every weekend my mom would call me up and I would be busy having drinks with friends from work. I worried that if I hung out with my family too much, my friendships would suffer. I was an idiot. Spending time with my mother is special, because if you've ever met her, you would know that her favorite activity is to make fun of me. It's endearing when she does it, because I know she misses me. Being around family once in a while gives me the love and support I need to forget about all the rough patches at work. Who knew that a home-cooked meal could be the perfect antidote to creating 154 soul-sucking PowerPoint slides?

I JOINED TWITTER

I worried that I would miss the opportunity to know what's happening in the world when I was tied to my desk for eight hours a day. Luckily, I discovered Twitter, which connected me with other like-minded people who just wanted the clock to move a little faster. It's also a huge reason I ended up working in social media management for most of my clients. Thanks, Internet.

I TOOK A SICK DAY WHEN I WASN'T SICK

My mother told me I was born exactly at 8 A.M., which is probably why I wake up every morning at 7 A.M. kicking and screaming. Pair that with working late nights in the office and you've got the perfect recipe for a girl who's burnt the fuck out. One day I decided to take one for myself and call in "sick." We've all done it, the fake cough, the raspy voice, the AAAAACHOOO! SORRY! And honestly? It was great. There was a little aunty voice in my head calling me lazy for the first couple of hours, but I've learned to ignore it.

ACTUAL 100 PERCENT TOTALLY NOT MADE UP THINGS A BROWN PERSON HAS HEARD AT THE OFFICE

It is tough being a person of color. It is absolutely 1,000 percent tougher being a person of color in a corporate environment. I've held countless jobs in countless offices where I was the only brown girl at the agency. And for whatever reason I was never allowed to forget it either. Here are a few very real things I have heard during my time in corporate hell:

"WOULD YOU LIKE SOME BUTTER CHICKEN?"
(said in a very "Apu accent")

The Apu accent is an evergreen tool used by the casual corporate racist to put down those that season their food. My family did not endure three wars and a genocide for me to sit quietly while some idiot bobbled his head in attempts to "playfully" bond with his new Indian coworker.

"YEAH, NO OFFENSE, BUT I DON'T REALLY DATE BROWN GIRLS."

This comment—wildly inappropriate on at least fifty levels—was hurled in my direction when my Polish coworker decided to download Tinder and came across someone he referred to as "one of your people." Yuck.

"THAT'S GREAT, BUT CAN YOU ADD YOUR CULTURAL TWIST TO IT?"

This little gem came from a creative director when I was writing commercials at a massive global advertising agency. Remember, being brown in the workplace is only useful to the extent your employer can monetize it.

"CAN YOU RECOMMEND ANY GOOD INDIAN RESTAURANTS IN THE AREA?"

One little-known fact is that my middle name is actually Yelp and I spend half my days researching Indian restaurants in every neighborhood on the planet. Don't believe me? Just utter this little racist blurb and find out. By the way, I usually just suggest the first restaurant that comes up on Google.

"DID YOU BRING SAMOSAS FOR THE POTLUCK? I WAS EXPECTING SAMOSAS!"

If the examples above weren't enough to get me to practice rolling out of moving cars to avoid these conversations, this was the one that sealed the deal. One word, Brad? You realized that I am from the same culture that made samosas? Where is my jar of mayonnaise, Brad? I was expecting a jar of homemade mayo to dip these samosas in! This potluck is RUINED!

"CAN YOU MAKE IT A LITTLE MORE MAINSTREAM?"

Despite the fact that Canada is one of the most multicultural countries in the world, everything I pitched had to be tinkered with to become more digestible to a whiter audience. This was a response I came to expect. It was feedback I received all the time and an infuriating reminder of the lack of representation not only in the media but in the industries that try to sell things to consumers of that media (which aren't all white people). *Mainstream* in this sense simply meant "not your people." Not to worry, though. There are a billion of us. Sooner or later, we'll hook up with China and become the global mainstream.

"DID YOU MEET AJAY IN ACCOUNTING? HE'S INDIAN, TOO! YOU'LL GET ALONG!"

Look, I'm sure Ajay is a great guy. And I might even get along with him better than with the idiot who is attempting to lump me together with the other brown person at the workplace. But, no, we do not all have a secret handshake and, no, we're not going to find out we're cousins. Ajay could very well be an asshole, Brad. It is rude to assume things.

HOW I FAILED AND SUCCEEDED

I GOT FIRED ONCE

I was fired from my job after four years in a career I didn't love. I feared breaking this news to my family as I braced for the judgment, disappointment, and resulting theatrics that come with sharing a deeply personal failure. Failure isn't something we're taught to deal with, much less embrace, in our culture. Those who fail at their careers especially are shunned and talked about in whispers as if they'd committed a crime.

I THOUGHT I WAS GETTING PROMOTED

I burnt out and started worrying more about how I was going to keep myself from shoving a pencil through my brain every day. Thankfully, I was called into a meeting one Wednesday morning and got fired. My first boss told me that I had so much more to offer to the world and that I should move on to explore bigger and better options—to "go out there" and make my mark on the world. I'm almost certain now that she probably said those things to keep me from crying, but it was just what I needed to hear. It was as if she'd read my mind and picked the warmest, brightest, sunniest day of the week to deliver the good news. I wasn't sure how I was going to pay rent that month, but I was finally free.

After getting fired I began to draw again. I did not share either of these developments with my mother. When we spoke I would either avoid the subject of work entirely or refer to my artwork as "a project for a potential client." That client was me, and that project was a collection of cartoon aunties crying over burnt roti. What I couldn't explain to my mother was that I needed the space to figure out what I genuinely loved doing. And it turns out that I loved making art, which had been the case since I was born.

I took on three more advertising projects to pay my bills and not die, before realizing that my corporate gig was now the distraction from what I really wanted to do with my life: create more art. In a weird way, my firing was one of the first failures that taught me how to succeed. But the most dangerous part about falling in love with art (or any nontraditional profession) as a desi is explaining this to our families and enduring the fights that follow. In order to succeed in the arts, I had to sacrifice stability, and no desi parent wants to hear that. Same goes for entrepreneurship. So many of us move through life picking careers out of a hat and settling for a lifestyle that may not be suited for us in the name of what's safe.

I WAS BROKE FOR A LITTLE WHILE

Even though I had been fired and should have been in a state of panic because I had no financial backup, the habit of living frugally stuck with me since college (and, of course, from growing up in an immigrant home). I knew how to stretch $20 over a week and implement survival tactics my mother used when we were new to the country. At the time of my firing, I had just enough money to survive in downtown Toronto for four months. I put myself on unemployment insurance and received a few hundred dollars short of my rent and still found a way to buy art supplies. I was so in love with what I was creating that I made some dents in my credit to make it happen. If I had the choice, I would do it all over again.

I reminded myself that the freedom I have is far more rewarding than the approval of someone impressed by big, corporate-sounding titles. I eventually trademarked and copyrighted my work and began to invest more time in my art, and when I launched my website in 2015, I slowly stopped worrying about eating cereal for dinner three nights in a row.

I EARNED MY FIRST DOLLAR

The first sale I ever made by myself was forced on me by a very kind person who yelled at me on social media to make prints so they could give me their money. Thank you, order number 0001. I learned very quickly that being an artist is a whole different ball game once you're online. You instantly become disconnected from reality and begin to see yourself as others see you—for me, it was perfect. Since I had spent so much time making creative campaigns to push other, bigger brands, I figured it was time to apply that same knowledge to myself. I pretended that I was no different from the coffee shop selling Italian soda on the radio or the big brewery that made Super Bowl commercials year after year to sell the same shit. I started focusing on consistency and brand management of my art, and it turns out all those years being chained to an ad agency desk paid off in the real world. And in this world, I decided how much I got paid.

EVERYONE YELLED AT ME FOR A LITTLE BIT

Since I was pursuing my own business and I was the first one in the family to do so, it was inevitable that I would receive unwanted criticism about every professional decision. Working from home is also a unique burden because I was always mistaken for someone who doesn't actually work but is pursuing a hobby. It was necessary for me to have a thick skin. Being self-employed for such a long period of time got me so bummed out that I became depressed for a little bit. All those "what-ifs" came circling back to me. "What if this doesn't work out?" "What if you stay broke forever?" "What if you've failed Mom and Dad?!" "You should have just stayed in the office!" "Why bother fighting for this? You're not a good enough artist!" "You've lost your chance!"

Heavy stuff. But I had so many orders to ship and an exhibit on the way, so I channeled all my feelings into my paintings. Eventually, a year or two passed and I made it out alive, printing and wrapping orders, putting on exhibits and traveling with my friends. People eventually got tired of yelling at me, and started paying attention. It's naturally what happens when you block out the negativity.

You do not have to aim for anyone's approval; if your work is really your passion, chances are you have the drive to make it your occupation, too. It won't be easy, but it's the best gift you can give yourself. Don't worry, Author Aunty believes in you.

PART 3
LOVE

HO
VE

OH SHIT, ANDREW!
HIDE! MY DAD'S HOME

THE TIME I HID A GUY IN MY CLOSET

I dated a Guyanese boy once. It lasted a whole two weeks. I spotted him in the hallway in the eleventh grade on my way from skipping gym class (as usual). He was tall and slim and wore a XXXL white tee paired with a backwards fitted hat and Timberlands. He looked like a nineties hip-hop music video on legs and I was ALL ABOUT IT. Was he smart? Kind? I didn't know or care. Back then, us brown girls didn't have much opportunity to see ourselves in Western media, so I often gravitated to what seemed like the closest representation of myself and at that time it was hip-hop. Most of us grew up with hip-hop and pretended that we were the "five foot five caramel shorty with the brown eyes" all the hot guys rapped about. Naturally, I wanted this Guyanese dude to be the Ja Rule to my Ashanti, the P Diddy to my JLo, the LL Cool J to my girl in the LL Cool J "Hush" video. I immediately asked my best friend to grab his number for me (or to give mine; I'm not sure what my game was back then, but it worked every time).

After getting his digits, I flipped my phone and dialed him that night. We made an instant connection: he said, like, three words and I was all, "YEAH, WHATEVER, TAKE ME OUT ON A DATE TOMORROW AT LUNCH, OKAY? THANKS!" And just like that, lunchtime became our date hour. Every day at noon, Young LL Cool J and I would hang out by the football field or take a walk in the forest nearby. Our conversations didn't consist of anything remotely genuine, romantic, or meaningful. I was sixteen, and I only cared about a boy when he bought me food.

One afternoon on our lunch date, I told Young LL Cool J that I could whoop his ass in any video game. And since I am an absolute nerd, I could. He, being a stubborn, stupid boy, took me up on that challenge. He repeatedly pushed my buttons and kept pestering me about how girls can't game and that I was really talking about video games only to impress him. I saw red. I had to prove him wrong and defeat him in every video game possible that very day.

We went back to my house, which was located about five minutes from school. Both of us giggling and challenging each other, fantasizing about how good it would feel to win against the other person. As we approached the house, I warned him to keep his ears open for any noises in case my parents decided to come home. Like every other brown girl on the planet, I was not allowed to bring boys over to the house. If I was dying and I called for an ambulance in my family's absence, and the paramedic happened to be a man, I would have to refuse the help and bleed out slowly in our living room. Boys were (and still might be) a BIG NO-NO!

Young LL and I made our way upstairs into the guest room, where my Nintendo GameCube sat, still glistening from being freshly unpacked. At that time, this was one of the most popular gaming systems and I could not wait to show this guy how amazing I was at every one of the games I owned. I grabbed the controllers and turned on the console, and the two of us began to share a genuine moment. I sensed vulnerability, anger, excitement, and happiness between us. But this was right before I won at the first game and concluded that this guy wasn't worth dating because he sucked at racing.

As we continued to have one of our best (and last) dates ever, I heard the door unlock. Both of us paused and looked at each other. Hearts racing.

"Did you hear that?" I whispered.

"Yeah, what do I do?!" he asked.

"MARIA! Are you home?!" I heard a deep voice from downstairs. It was my father. He had decided to come home for lunch that day. SHIT!

"QUICK!" I pushed Young LL. "Go in my room and hide in the closet!"

"YES, DAD, I'M HERE!" I yelled back as I shoved Guyana boy between rows of sweaters and T-shirts and began to close the old wooden doors on his face.

"WHO ARE YOU WITH? WHOSE SHOES ARE THESE?!" I hear another yell from downstairs. This MORON had left his shoes at the front door! How was I supposed to cover this one up?! I began to panic.

"THEY'RE STEPHANIE'S GYM SHOES, DAD. SHE TOLD ME TO HOLD ON TO THEM FOR NEXT CLASS!!" Quality bullshitting, in my opinion.

"THESE ARE MEN'S SHOES," my father yelled back.

"SHE HAS BIG FEET," I said.

"OKAY, I WILL DROP YOU BACK TO SCHOOL ONCE I AM DONE WITH MY LUNCH, OKAY?" My father knew something wasn't right, but he knew that whatever was happening upstairs couldn't be left up there if we all decided to leave.

OR SO HE THOUGHT.

"Okay, I'm sorry for shoving you into a closet, but you have to listen to me and LISTEN CLOSELY." I grabbed him by the shoulders and shook him as I whispered like an army general in hiding. "On this piece of paper, I have written down the code to disarm the security system. If anything begins to beep or ring, punch this in and MAKE A RUN FOR IT! Do NOT spend one extra second in this house once we leave. As soon as you hear that garage door close, you HAVE to run downstairs and get out."

He was quiet. He smiled and nodded.

"What about my shoes?!" he whispered back.

"They're downstairs. Take them. Or I can just bring them for you. JUST GET OUT OF THE HOUSE FIRST, OKAY???"

I heard a knock on my bedroom door.

"MARIA! Are you okay in there?! Are you ready to go?" My father was so close on the other side of the door that I was afraid he could smell the DECEPTION.

"YES, DAD! JUST CHANGING. We will leave in FIVE MINUTES!" I said loud enough so that closet boy could hear the plan.

"OKAY, I WILL BE WAITING DOWNSTAIRS FOR YOU," my father yelled once more through the door. At this point I was having a full-on panic attack with this guy hiding in my closet.

I gathered my things and ran downstairs to the car.

"Let's go! I'm going to be late for class, Dad!" I tried to rush him out of the house.

"Oh, one second, I forgot something inside," my father said as he went back into the house.

OH SHIT, OH SHIT, OH SHIT.

WHAT IF HE HAD COME OUT OF THE CLOSET ALREADY? WHAT IF HE WAS MAKING HIS WAY DOWN? WHAT IF, WHAT IF, WHAT IF?

I flipped my phone and began to text him: "DO NOT LEAVE YET!"

Just a few seconds later, my father gets back into the car, a bottle of water in hand. A rush of relief and joy washed over me and I leaned back into the seat.

The car exits the garage and the door begins to close. I text Guyanese boy again: "OK, LEAVE NOW!"

I started laughing and texting all my girlfriends about what had gone down, excited that I pulled this off and no one got hurt! As we rolled up to the school, I said goodbye and ran into the school lobby to meet my friends and explain my near-death experience in full detail. The bell rang at that moment and we all walked into our last classes of the day.

Ten minutes into the class, my mind began to wander. Guyana boy hadn't texted me back and my anxiety grew at the thought of my father finding him in our house. I had begun writing him a text when my name was announced over the school's PA.

"Can Maria Quarmarel please come down to the principal's office. Maria Quamreal. Thank you."

Oh, good. Maybe he had returned to tell me the story of his epic escape in person. Maybe he wasn't as stupid as I thought! And maybe, just maybe I could go on one more date with him. I was filled with hope. Unfortunately for my idiot naive self, it was not Guyana boy who was standing at the doors of my high school, it was my dad. And he looked PISSED.

FFFFFFFFFFFUUUUUUUUUUUUUUUUUUUUUUUUUUUCCCCKKK!

"Hi, Dad . . . " I nervously approached him.

"Get. In. The. Car. Now." His eyes were wide with rage as he muttered through his teeth, grinding them as if he had just popped an ecstasy.

"What happened?" I asked, pretending I didn't kidnap and hold a Guyanese refugee in our home.

To this this day I'm not sure exactly what happened in my house during the first ten minutes of class, but it was explained that Guyana boy took FIFTEEN FRIGGIN' MINUTES (the drive to school and most of the duration of the class I attended) to leave my house. WHAT WAS HE DOING IN THERE FOR THAT LONG?! GOING THROUGH MY UNDERWEAR DRAWER?

My father had found him sneaking out of the front door as he was pulling up to the driveway, and proceeded to grab his shoes from the doorway and chase him through the neighborhood with them. Everyone involved was traumatized for life and I never went home for lunch again. I also never heard from Guyana boy again ever, but I know that he got out alive. I just never followed up with him to figure out why he took so long to leave. If you're reading this, Young LL Cool J, it was your fault. All of this trouble and you didn't even win a single game. You can't be sexist, bad at video games, AND bad at sneaking out of houses. I hope you learned your lesson.

SHE'S TALKING TO BOYS! WE'RE RUINED!

SPICE METER

8 out of 10 green chilies. Relationships are tough. The aunty buffer is tougher.

CHARACTERISTICS

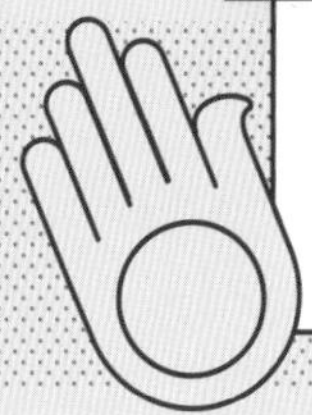

Matchmaker aunty is the human version of Tinder. She's got a roster of single and marginally single boys and girls who unwittingly have confessed to her that they are on the market. She will now try to set you up with all of them.

WHERE YOU MIGHT FIND THEM

Outside of the typical fam jam scenario, you can find an MM aunty in temples/mosques/churches, chatting up your folks about the Chappalwala boy who just graduated with a degree in engineering and has great hair.

STRENGTHS

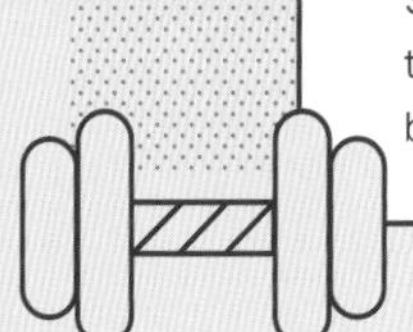

She can hook you up with the best plumber in town, or the tailor who can make Sabyasachi quality sarees for cheap back home, but not in the way you'd like her to.

WEAKNESSES

While this aunty has many strengths, matchmaking is not one of them. You can be sure of having the best worst-first-date stories to share with your girlfriends if you take a chance on the MM aunty.

SCENARIO I

SHE TELLS YOU TO SPEAK TO HER MARRIED SON ABOUT HIS BEST FRIEND AND PHD CANDIDATE, ARJUN.

ROOKIE MOVE

Speak with her son and ask about Arjun. Arjun isn't interested in you or any woman. Arjun just wants to be left alone. You can relate to this. You respect this.

BOSS MOVE

Upon finding out that you and Arjun are both just victims of a nosy aunty, you become friends. You help shield each other from the plotting of your aunties while both keeping an eye out for each other's TRUE BOLLYWOOD HERO.

OH, RANBIR...

SCENARIO II

MM AUNTY JUST INTERRUPTED YOUR KARAOKE-NIGHT PLANS AND INVITED THE CHAPPALWALAS TO COME FOR DINNER.

ROOKIE MOVE

Be yourself, see where this goes. You're still in your third year of college with no idea of how you're going to continue living off ramen for the next little while, but maybe throwing an extravagant wedding with the negative balance in your bank account is the answer.

BOSS MOVE

Show up dressed for karaoke night. Politely say your hellos and goodbyes. Invite the son to join you on your way out. You have just made a new friend.

YOUR PARTY LOOKS BORING AND YOUR SAMOSAS LOOK STALE!

WHERE'S MY SHAH RUKH?

I've always been a huge believer in romance. Oh, what would I do without it?! I remember being six and watching all the rom-coms with Shah Rukh and Amir and Arjun and wishing I were the beautiful girl they would serenade with five to six songs in an hour. I would run around in the hallways of our closed-off Gujarati colony and pretend I was frolicking among lush trees and beautiful flowers, trying to find my love dancing on the other end. The fantasy of having a man fall so deeply in love with me at first sight who was also actually someone I thought was supercool right back gave me hope for an eventual happily ever after.

In my teens I held on to that fantasy and dated guys that would profess the simplest romantic idea, because that's how it worked in movies. Oh, you like my shirt? Let's date! Oh, you think I'm funny in class? Let's go get ice cream! You like my laugh? I don't ever remember laughing around you, but fuck it! It's cute! Let's date! I always latched onto the smallest things because I genuinely believed it was the start of my love story—that this sixteen-year-old fuddu* who stole Hennessy out of his dad's liquor cabinet to look cool was my Shah Rukh. At that age, I couldn't tell when a boy was being sincere or was just using pickup tactics.

Needless to say, they all failed. We would talk on the phone for hours, go hiking in the woods so I could impose a romantic setting like a lush green field onto our encounter, and go months without kissing because that was a HUGE deal. In old school Bollywood, kissing happened only in our imaginations after the movie ended. Kissing wasn't ever shown during the duration of the entire three-hour epic romance. Anything more than a hand's graze across a girl's bare stomach was taboo, and not the kind of love I was taught

*Fool.

KISS ME, MALIKA...
BUT YOU SMELL LIKE DARU!

to seek. It was embarrassingly difficult to find a boy who cared for me in the way Bollywood heroes did. And as a result, I slowly began to see myself as less of a heroine.

Through the tears and heartache I would find solace and comfort in watching more Bollywood, with each film delivering a different, cheesier way to fall in love than the last. What if I find him at a bus stop, or maybe I would bump into him on a busy street, accidentally spilling coffee all over his shirt. Maybe he saw me shopping through a store window and fell head over heels, or maybe we've known each other all our lives and he finally just had to say something. My mind would race with all of the possibilities of romance that I had yet to explore. I bought tarot cards and checked whether my sign was compatible with other astrological signs (even though I still know fuck all about it—I think I'm the fish one). I would hurt myself in the process because I still felt that I was doing something wrong; that the reason I couldn't find love at first sight was because I wasn't someone worth loving at first sight. I also realized that, unlike in the movies, I needed an actual, meaningful conversation to fall in love, even though Aishwarya never had to deal with that shit.

I eventually began rejecting the idea that the man sitting across from me would propose at the end of the night because the way I ordered thirteen entrées would drive him crazy with love. I became someone who didn't give a flying chappal if he found me attractive. I began to have a good time not picturing myself as the damsel in distress because deep down, I didn't want to be saved. This isn't to say that the proposals rolled in like that scene from *Harry Potter* where Hogwarts blasted Harry's house with invitations. But it did mean that I was finally free to reject love at first sight. And I did.

I rejected men online, I rejected them on the street, I rejected them over the phone. I was rejecting so much I started to believe that I was the hero, looking for someone I would fall in love with first. It felt great. I began to take charge of where I would go to eat, how much space I needed, how much support I was willing to give and accept, and ultimately how and when I was ready to take things seriously. The hardest part about dating while desi is rejecting the idea of a surprise love, of a lifelong commitment blossoming with someone you've spent two hours with. It's the stupid Bollywood narrative we love to indulge in that becomes hurtful when compared to our real lives. There are no Bollywood films about your potential partner earning less money than you, or the tension that might come from asking your husband to sacrifice his career to become a stay-at-home dad. There are no Bollywood songs about what happens when you get cheated on by your arranged fiancé, or about abuse or coming out to your parents.

The love of your life won't be the lunatic that proposes to you the fastest. It'll be your best friend who understands the incredible obstacles you will face together as partners, lovers, and maybe parents.

I've let go of my dreams of finding Mr. Right at the traffic light, and embraced my freedom to choose what is really right for me. I still enjoy the corniest of romantic scenarios conjured by our lovely cinema to explode our ovaries. I still pretend that young Amitabh Bachchan is standing on the other side of every verdant field I walk through. I still imagine what it would be like to have a band serenading me with cute songs to win my heart. But I know that one day I will create my own romantic comedy with someone who cherishes me enough to commit to a cheesy gesture, but also supports me in tangible ways that go beyond flowers and candy. And for the first time in a long time, I am excited to fall in love again.

THE SOFT AUNTY
JEETAY RAHO, BETA!
SPICE RATING?
1/10
SPICE METER
1 out of 10 green chilies. Mild like malai, and the only time the acronym TSA would ever stand for something good.

CHARACTERISTICS

You know that one aunty in every soap opera who was the good guy? Yeah, that one. That's the soft aunty. She's your friend. A little intrusive, a little pushy, but always the first one to give her blessing. Her tag line is "JEETE RAHO, PUTTAR!" (meaning "Stay winning, kid!").

WHERE YOU MIGHT FIND THEM

The soft aunty is omnipresent; she is the one lady in every uncomfortable scenario who hates everyone in the room as much as you do—and will say something lighthearted to ease the tension or take unwanted attention away from you.

STRENGTHS

The soft aunty is called soft for a reason; she gives fantastic hugs. She also repeatedly uses the words *bechari*, *bholi*, and *bachhi* to your parents so they are always reminded that you are innocent and would never do anything suspicious ever.

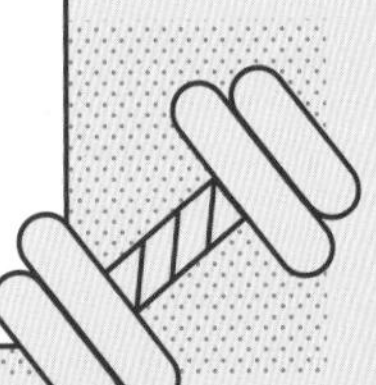

WEAKNESSES

Your stupidity is her weakness. She's worked so long and hard to paint this holy picture of you in front of everyone and you went ahead and BETRAYED HER TRUST by GETTING AN ASTROLOGICAL SIGN TATTOOED ON YOUR NECK?!

SCENARIO 1

YOU INTRODUCE YOUR NON-DESI BOYFRIEND TO THE FAMILY.

ROOKIE MOVE

Teach him five Hindi words before introducing him yourself and pray he doesn't get roasted at dinner.

BOSS MOVE

Introduce him to soft aunty first, which will go something like "We don't know what you guys eat over there, but it must be good because you, son, have great taste." Then let her take the lead in introducing Brad to the rest of the family.

I DIDN'T MOVE FROM BOMBAY FOR THIS BULLSHIT!

SCENARIO II

YOU'VE JUST BROKEN UP WITH YOUR HARAMI BOYFRIEND.

ROOKIE MOVE

Sit quietly and wait until the hurt passes. Confide only in your close friends and pretend he never existed.

BOSS MOVE

Tell soft aunty EVERYTHING. You will never regret this decision, as TSA will comfort you with endless soft hugs and delicious food and will put on her PETTY AUNTY HAT to deliver just the right amount of low blows to make you go, "Yeah, you're right, Aunty, HE WASN'T all that! I DO deserve better, and you know what? I WILL have another scoop of mango ice cream while watching *Kuch Kuch Hota Hai* with you!"

YOU'RE SUCH A FOOL! HOW COULD YOU FALL IN LOVE WITH ANOTHER NIKAMMA?!

MY BETI IS THE BEST BETI!

OH, JAANU, YOU'RE NOT A DOCTOR, BUT I LOVE YOU!

HOW TO FLIRT WITH A DESI GIRL

Rather than try to give you advice about how to flirt with a desi girl (after all, we're all different), I thought I'd share some real messages from my inbox that best exemplify the art of seduction.

"HIIII HEY BAES LUKIN2 HOT IN DA PIC. . . . NEWAY WHR R U FRM. . . . U LUK LIKE AN INDIAN BUT UR NAME DOESN'T SOUND LIK ONE. . . . NEWAY BIIIII. . . . TC. . . . . N PLZ REPLY."

—Facebook user, India

"I LV UR EYESSSSS. . . . THEY R JUZ SOOOOOOOO SEXYYYYYYYY."

—Saim, 40, Bangalore

"YOU KNOW YOU ARE RARE QUALITY \>\>\>\> YOU HAVE SHOWN YOU CAN LOOK GOOD WITHOUT EXPOSING UR SELF."

—Mas, 55, Pakistan

"SALAM I HOPE ALL IS FINE, MY NAME IS ASHER I LIVE IN LONDON I AM SINGLE PROFESSIONAL. MY FAMILY ORIGIN IS FROM UAE. WE ARE SEARCHING FOR A GOOD GIRL . . . GIRL FROM A EDUCATED BACKGROUND AND THIS TIME THOUGHT WHY NOT TRY THE FB SOCIAL NETWORKING SO I RANDOMLY SECHED THE FB AND LIKE UR PROFILE THAT'S WHY I AM MESSAGING YOU. PLEASE WE ARE LOOKING FOR A . . . PROFESSIONAL EDUCATED GIRL FROM A GOOD FAMILY FOR MARRIAGE PROPOSAL. IF U R SINGLE OR SEARCHING PLEASE DO CONTACT ME I AM A BRITISH-EUROPEAN CITIZEN."

—Dr. Asher, 30, UK

"HI DASHHHHN WUSPP? CRE TO B FRANDSHIP?!"

—Shoeaz, 28, India

I hope you learned something. I'm rooting for you.

HEY, BBY,
LET'S SÁX TONÍTE...
LEAVE ME
ALONE, PLS.

TYPES OF PEOPLE I'VE DATED

THE MAMA'S BOY

MERE PAAS... MA HAI!

This is a package deal. You won't get through a single conversation without this guy mentioning his mother. He thinks this is charming and will make him seem like a family-oriented dude, when it simply strengthens the stereotype that his mother probably does his laundry and takes the bones out of the fish before serving it to him. Try to turn down an invitation to the family dinner within the first few dates. You don't want Auntyji hunting you down if this all goes south.

I WOULD NEVER GO TO KHANDALA!

THE RICH KID

Our people have a very special ability to completely blow things out of proportion. The Rich Kid particularly suffers from this problem. He's the guy who shows up in the most expensive car, holding a bouquet of at least a thousand roses and a diamond necklace on the first date. The only downside to this is you might not be the only girl having breakfast at Tiffany's that week.

BIRTHDAY?! ON LEG DAY?!!

THE BEEFCAKE

Put that parantha down, because it's time to hit the gym for the third time this afternoon. The Beefcake will make you want to take up rock-climbing just so you can jump him properly. He's supersweet and loving, but will probably serve you unseasoned chicken breasts for dinner every night.

THE BOLLYWOOD HERO

What the hell is up with that hair? Why is it so poofy? Who wears it like that anymore? Is that a mesh tank top with a bandana around the neck? Why does he slur his Hindi words like he's perpetually drunk? Why does he stutter when he says your name? Oh, right. This guy is way too Bollywood. He's great for catching a few movies and playing B-wood trivia, but you're just not his Paro.

THE GOD-LOVER

Do you like wearing lace bras as tops? Then forget about this one. Your God-loving boo will have you censoring curse words and throwing back holy water at the club. He doesn't believe in dating outside the religion but will probably do a lot of things in the sack that will make you want to convert. (I'm going to hell for this one.)

THE RIGHT ONE

Could be any of the above, could be none, or could be all. You'll never know until you go out there and explore. For me, it's a mix between the Bollywood Hero and the Beefcake. Although I've been known to date a lotta Rich Kid/Mama's Boy types. I had one great outing with a God-Lover, but that didn't turn out so hot when he said he'd "fight" to have me accepted. NO THANK YOU.

DATE SPOTS THAT WON'T GET YOU BUSTED

The sky is blue, water is wet, and desis have the hardest time going on a date because aunties are on the creep 24/7. These are facts. This is science. Call up Bill Nye if you don't believe me. Growing up desi meant having to hide every phase of my dating life while sneaking dates disguised as study groups and late-night work sessions. Dating is even harder when you're living at home. Here are a few date spots that won't get you busted by aunties and ruin your chances of getting to third base with Anand.

- ***A Nicaraguan restaurant:*** No real reason for an aunty to be here. Unless you're Nicaraguan. In that case, go to an Indian restaurant.
- ***A nude beach:*** I actually had this deep feeling of fear as I wrote this one out. I am 99.9 percent sure you won't encounter an aunty here, but God help us all if you do.
- ***Chanel store:*** There is no way in hell Auntyji is paying $3,000 for a bag she can acquire from India for 3,000 rupees. Have some champagne and window-shop with bae all you want. Maybe make out in the dressing rooms if you're feeling classy.
- ***Korean grill:*** You think aunty will come all this way to cook her own food? WITHOUT MASALA? You're definitely in the clear here. Play footsie under the burner.
- ***Cat café:*** A true aunty would never insert herself in a situation where all she can think about is cleaning. Share a dessert with your soul mate and purr along with your furry friends in peace.

- ***Skydiving:*** These date ideas are getting weird. But that's a good thing. You'll be free of private eyes 10,000 feet in the air, or at least too fast for them to catch a glimpse. Strap yourself to your partner and take a leap of faith. You won't hear CHI-CHI from up here.
- ***Salsa class:*** Aside from a few cougars here and there, you won't experience much aunty activity here. And it's hot as hell. Soon you'll be the cougar aunty here. Full circle.

If all of these ideas fail, you can always do what we do at desperate times in the suburbs: McDonald's Drive Thru and chill. Good luck, and remember, you were always at the library with Preeti.

WHAT TO LOOK FOR IN AN ARRANGED HUSBAND/PARTNER

In this day and age, being arranged simply means that your mother is playing Tinder with your biodata. So if you're going to go down that route, you gotta at least know what to look for. Are they fit? Do they smell weird? Are they dating someone already and are too afraid to tell Mummy and Daddy? Here's what I would suggest to add to that checklist.

- ☑ Respects women (and not in a because-this-could-be-my-sister-or-mother kinda way)
- ☑ Can accept defeat without blaming your "luck" (even if you were lucky)
- ☑ Knows all of the words to at least one Bollywood smash hit (which will evidently be played at least three times during your wedding)
- ☑ Arjun Rampal
- ☑ Solid knowledge of Drake's discography
- ☑ NO DAD JEANS
- ☑ Can talk about politics for a good three and a half hours (with your father)
- ☑ Can cook biryani
- ☑ Doesn't laugh at you when you drunkenly get your *v*'s and *w*'s mixed up
- ☑ Supports your decision to become famous as hell
- ☑ Enjoys your food and asks for thirds
- ☑ Eats rice with his hands like a true desi because he knows how much better it tastes
- ☑ Calls your mom "Mummy"
- ☑ Is super lush and hairy so you can pet him when you're stressed out
- ☑ Loves you like Shah Rukh loves Paro

HELLO! IT'S BEEN THREE DATES, ASHISH! WHERE THE HELL IS MY RING?!

MY IDEAL BOLLYWOOD MOVIE

I'm a twentysomething workaholic still trying to figure my shit out. I live in a cute minimalist apartment with a white roommate who loves all my little desi quirks, doesn't mind that the house always smells like lauki daal, and gives me insight into dating. She's consistently baffled by the fact that my family would never allow their daughter to roam around with a boyfriend. She insists that they need to learn to accept me for who I am. But really she's ignorant and forgets that I am in fact not white, and shit doesn't work that way. I work a sedentary nine-to-five job doing something mundane like filing or writing ads, and I have a smokin' hot body and can eat whatever I want. My parents are not in the picture because they're always out on cute little cruises and enjoy every minute they have away from me.

CUE

SONG-AND-DANCE BIT WHERE ROOMIE AND I DISCUSS WHY I HIDE LITERALLY EVERY PART OF MY SOCIAL LIFE FROM MY FAMILY. (HINT: IT'S BECAUSE I'M TERRIFIED THEY WILL DISOWN ME.)

He's a super-rich Hot Hero Guy (HHG) who probably inherited his parents' wealth because he's the most responsible out of his three equally hot brothers. The family business is some type of holding company. But despite his wealth and great looks, he is emotionally unfulfilled due to the lack of love and support he receives from his immediate family. Nobody ever really knows what he's up to because he likes to keep a low profile, but he has a few close friends and they're all supportive and not idiots. This entire description is problematic; I am well aware of this.

CUE

SONG-AND-DANCE NUMBER WITH HOT HERO GUY IN HIS BOARDROOM, AFTER A SUCCESSFUL PITCH WITH HIS COWORKERS, SINGING ABOUT HOW HE HAS EVERYTHING HE'S EVER WANTED IN LIFE. EXCEPT A WIFE . . .

It's a bright and sunny day, and I'm going for a jog, looking fly as all hell. Passersby are turning their heads, looking at me, thinking, Damn, this girl looks like she has her life and her abs together. It's the golden hour and my silky, shimmering ponytail is bouncing as I am running in slow-mo when a fatal car crash occurs at an intersection I'm getting ready to cross. As the car engine bursts into flames, a chunk of debris flies in my direction, and with my instinctual feline reflexes, I dodge it. I then brush myself off and continue to inspect the scene along with the rest of the bystanders. It's a family in the car: mother, father, and a baby.

CUE

THE WHISPERS ABOUT MY CRAZY HEROIC FEAT SLOWLY TURN INTO A COOL LITTLE SONG REMINISCENT OF A YING YANG TWINS TRACK. (YOU KNOW WHICH ONE.)

"THERE'S A BABY IN THERE! MOVE!" I yell as I push everyone out of the way and sprint towards the explosion. Everyone is in awe.

I begin to smash the windows to save the baby (because obviously the parents died on impact). As this is all happening, cars begin to pile up behind the scene of the accident. For some reason, no rescuers—the police, ambulances, or the fire department—have shown up. Cars continue to form a tight gridlock when a man steps out of his car and begins to walk towards me. It's Hot Hero Guy. After witnessing the scene, he had told his driver to stop the car and let him out so he could help me save this baby. Both of us work together to get the baby out of the car. Then through the fire, smoke, debris, and destruction, we look at each other. We immediately fall in love and raise this baby as if it were our own—a completely unreal scenario that would never ever happen, but, hey, that's what makes it so Bollywood.

CUE

PEPPER IN A SONG WHILE WE'RE LOOKING INTO EACH OTHER'S EYES FOR, LIKE, THREE TO FIVE MINUTES. THIS ONE IS ABOUT HOW EVERYTHING IS FIGURATIVELY, AND LITERALLY, LIT.

"What about the conflict, Maria? You forgot the spicy drama that we all love!" you'll say. Obviously the drama would come from the fact that our parents will disapprove from all sides. His parents would hate me because I am not rich and have a baby out of wedlock. They do not know the full rescue story and immediately shun me.

CUE

SONG ABOUT HOW HHG HAS BEEN LIVING UNDER THE SHADOW OF HIS FAMILY, EVEN THOUGH HE'S THE ONE WHO THROUGH HIS HARD WORK KEEPS THEM ALL LIVING SO LAVISHLY. YET THEY WON'T GIVE HIM A CHANCE TO FOLLOW HIS DREAM OF BECOMING A STAY-AT-HOME DAD.

My family would disapprove because the baby is not mine, and they'd force me to return her or him to its family (which is absolutely the right thing to do

IRL, but that's not how my story is written, so everyone will have to suck it up). Both sides begin to fight by making petty jabs at the others' social status, marital issues, and education levels. Meanwhile, I'm with Hot Hero Guy flirting in baby yoga classes, pretending to be the perfect family. Strangers on the street compliment us on how adorable the three of us look, and HHG instantly gushes; he's obsessed with the idea and is set on marrying ya girl. And I'm 'bout it, 'cause he's a responsible dude.

SONG ABOUT HOW I'M 'BOUT IT.

Eventually, with the help of HHG's close friends, my wild-card roommate, and his hot brothers, we devise a plan to take the baby out of hiding in a nursery I had built in my apartment and tell our parents the truth. We trick the two families into joining us for a large dinner and tell them the story about how we found the baby and how it's adorable and not illegal to keep this baby as our own. We obviously have a lovable, too-open-minded-to-be-real grandmother standing by our side to vouch for us, and everyone will eventually approve and throw us a huge, lavish wedding. For convenience's sake, the baby isn't present for all of this. It will enter into the picture once we're married.

The film ends with a musical number in which everyone from both families is dancing to a GOAT disco/trap Indian wedding classic, including cameos from SRK, Ranbir Kapoor, Ranveer Singh, Deepika Padukone, Big B, Lil' B, Aishwarya Rai Bachchan, Aamir Khan, and Future.

I would call this film *I Love You, Baby!*, because it's corny enough to make me watch it in theaters. I'm looking forward to it already.

BEAUTY
BODY

AND
COLOR
PART 4

THE DESI WORKOUT
I STAY FIT BY CRYING TO MOTHER INDIA!

Hanji, hi, hello ji, thanks for attending the Desi Workout Power Hour. My name is Hatecopy and I will be your instructor for this evening. Tonight we are going to learn how to shed those parantha pounds and work on that ladoo booty. In our culture, we celebrate something new every day. And with the average desi family consisting of at least five hundred people, we've got weddings galore to keep us snackin' on those jalebis and shooting back gallons of dairylicious lassi. Now I'm no medical expert, but I'm pretty sure all of this will give you a heart attack.

We gotta take proper care of ourselves. So let's do it together. Twenty minutes of this simple workout every day will help you keep in shape and allow you to continue snacking without worrying about your blouse bursting in the middle of garba. What's even better is that you won't even know you're working out! How convenient!

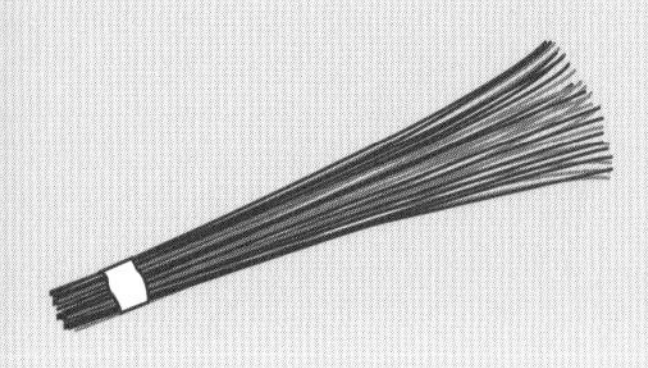

STEP 1: JHAROO

This is what we call a JHAROO. No, it's not a broom. Yes, that IS the handle. And, yes, you've got to bend down all the way to the ground and sweep that shit from side to side. This is a traditional way of cleaning the house in the motherland, and a GREAT core-strengthening exercise. Clean the whole house, make your mother proud, then make her unproud by flexing that eight-pack in your bikini.

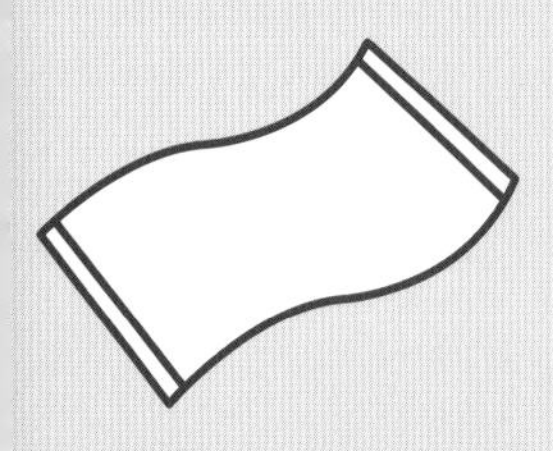

STEP 2: POCHA

What did you think? You were going to JHAROO without the POCHA?! You crazy? Get back down there!! Pocha is what we call MOPPING. But it is not done with a Swiffer, oh no. You've got to find any old rag—maybe an old T-shirt, a pillowcase, your grandpa's dhoti, whatever is close by—and mop the entire house with it. To do the pocha correctly, one must (again) get down to the ground and simply wipe the floors from side to side until every inch of the house is spotless. It is great for your biceps and core. It is also great for your butt because you're squatting for an extended period of time trying to get that damn turmeric stain out of the kitchen floor.

STEP 3: CRY

One healthy exercise you can practice from your couch is to watch *Mother India* and cry A LOT. This will be a great ab workout because the way you cry while watching that baby drown is the kind of sadness that comes from THE CORE. It will ruin you emotionally, but build you up physically. And since you'll be reaching for the tissues so many times, you'll get some upper body workout in there as well. You'll be crying for now, but your haters will be crying later when they see your sweet hot bod at the next Goan getaway.

STEP 4: SWEAR IN THE HOUSE

Go in the middle of the house and yell, "FUCK THIS SHIT!" and wait until you hear rapid thuds approaching in your direction. Now start running, because if one of your parents catches you, it is game over. This chase will probably involve your mother holding a weapon that will most definitely be used to whoop your butt into another dimension, so you have to make sure your pace is consistent. This is a great cardio workout and a very convenient way to practice self-defense. I do this workout almost daily. My family hates me, but my sweet abs do not.

SPICE METER

10 out of 10 green chilies. Just straight-up ruthless. You have been warned.

CHARACTERISTICS

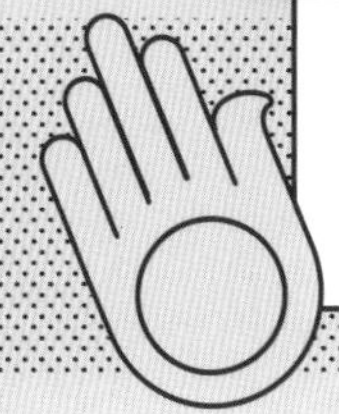

The weight-watcher aunty is almost never a spokesmodel for LA Fitness, but is always the first one to point out that you aren't either.

WHERE YOU MIGHT FIND THEM

YOU CAN ALWAYS FIND THEM HOVERING OVER YOUR SHOULDER AT THE WEDDING BUFFET. ALWAYS.

STRENGTHS

Knowing when to call you fat.

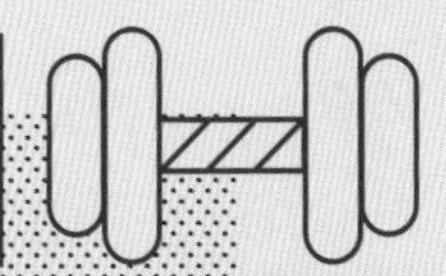

WEAKNESSES

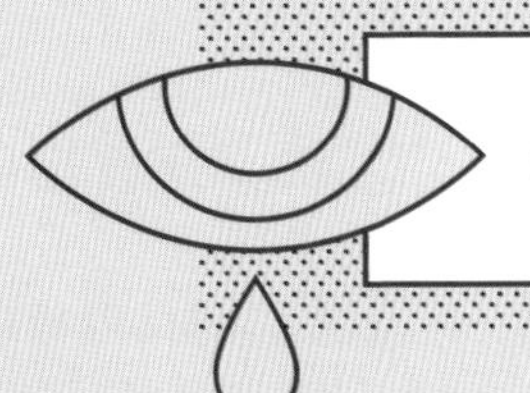

Not knowing when to stop calling you fat.

SCENARIO 1

YOU ARE AT A DINNER PARTY. YOU HAVE DECIDED TO GO FOR SECONDS. SHE YELLS, "YOU'RE GETTING A LITTLE MOTI IN THE ARMS!" OR "SLOW DOWN, BETI, YOU CAN EAT ALL YOU WANT AFTER MARRIAGE!"

ROOKIE MOVE

Put the plate down and wipe your tears with the stuffed animals at the kids' table.

BOSS MOVE

Take more food than you were about to. Tell her you want to be as HEALTHY as her. This will get you slapped, but it is so, so worth it.

YOUR DAUGHTER'S GETTING A LITTLE MOTI IN THE ARMS, NO?

SCENARIO II

YOU HAVE DECIDED TO MAKE CHANGES TO THE WAY YOU EAT BECAUSE IT WORKS BETTER WITH YOUR LIFESTYLE/FITNESS ROUTINE.

ROOKIE MOVE

Tell that to your aunty and get introduced for the next five years as the girl who's "on a white people diet."

BOSS MOVE

Tell no one. What you eat is your business despite what your aunty might tell you. Successfully avoid all samosas, look fabulous, and wear the skimpiest saree at the next function to show off your sweet, healthy, powerhouse bod.

I HEARD THE FOOD WAS SO BAD THAT SHE WENT ON A DIET!

SMART VS. HEALTHY

Aunties often use the code terms *healthy* and *smart* as a passive-aggressive way to comment on our body types. No one really knows why this is so, but it's always good to know.

HEALTHY
ANYTHING NOT SKINNY.
SMART
SKINNY.

I mean, does being slim mean you're not healthy? And are all healthy people idiots? Am I an idiot by this logic? This explains a lot. If you ask any ordinary desi girl, she will tell you that the smart/healthy comparison does not make or break a person, but it does frustrate the hell out of her. For example, you could be working out and building all sorts of muscle mass, but in the eyes of an aunty, you would be on the same level as someone like me, whose only exercise comes from brushing her extensions once a week. Sorry about that.

[CRIES IN CURRY]

ALL THE BENEFITS OF COCONUT OIL

The secret to unleashing your Indian fabulosity inside and out: COCONUT OIL. Contrary to popular non-desi belief, coconut oil is more than just a cooking agent. A lot of us grew up with that stuff in our hair before it ever reached our mouth. Here are a few benefits and uses of coconut oil, according to traditional desi practices.

Hair mask: While most girls had sleepovers and movie nights, we spent our nights having our scalps rigorously massaged with coconut oil by an aunty. This was to ensure that our hair grew long, strong, silky, and shiny. There's a reason why our people take pride in our manes; and genetics are deserving of only half that credit. Massage fistfuls of melted coconut oil into your hair from scalp to tip every week for luscious locks.

Deodorant: I'm DEAD serious. Coconut oil has antibacterial properties as well as cooling agents that get rid of all your stank. Rub a small amount under each pit and head on over to that date. You'll remind them of a piña colada.

Fountain of youth: You ever wonder how Shah Rukh Khan was able to play a sixteen-year-old in movies for the last forty years? COCONUT OIL. It is clinically proven to improve your complexion and skin elasticity. It also has agents to minimize scars and reduce the effects of aging. SLAP SOME ON and you're ready for your close-up. Forever.

Weight loss: Get off that treadmill and pick up a spoon because coconut oil is said to be a great weight-loss agent. Just two tablespoons a day can help you reduce some of that stubborn ladoo fat from the hips and get back into fitting in your favorite saree.

THE DESI GLUTEN-FREE DIET

THERE IS NO SUCH THING. YOU WILL EAT ROTI AND RICE WHETHER YOU LIKE IT OR NOT.

HALDI MASK RECIPE

Sometimes you gotta take care of your face. Lucky for you, our ancestors have left us with a thousand ways to do so. One of them, called the haldi mask, is often used on weddings and special occasions to create a brighter, more even complexion for the week ahead.

ALL YOU NEED

1 teaspoon haldi *(turmeric)*
1 tablespoon yogurt *(or 3 tablespoons milk with 2 tablespoons flour)*
½ tablespoon coconut oil

HOW TO APPLY

Haldi masks are possibly easier than boiling water. You simply mix all the ingredients together, apply generously to the face until you look like you're doing it wrong, then wait ten minutes before rinsing off with water.

WHAT YOU WILL END UP WITH

Beautiful, glowing skin that will make you look like you've been getting a good night's sleep your whole life. Continue this once a week for everlasting desi radiance.

FAIR 'N' LOVELY

UNFAIR 'N' LOVELY

There was a drama that aired on desi cable channels across the West called *Saat Phere* (meaning "Seven Rounds," a reference to a traditional Hindu marital ceremony). It featured a girl named Saloni who faces all sorts of bullshit obstacles because she was born a shade or two darker than her siblings. As I caught an episode with my mother, I asked, "Ma, why is it such a big deal that she's darker?" The response was a look that said, "That was a stupid question, Maria." And it was stupid, because I was so incredibly blind to shadism in desi culture.

Unlike Saloni, I was born fair-skinned, with jet-black curly hair; I was often referred to as gori* or guriya because I resembled the white dolls I always used to play with. I remember young girls from all over the neighborhood would come over and beg my mother to let them carry me around and show me off. Girls we didn't even know would offer to babysit and dress me up, even line up to take pictures with me on birthdays. I was everyone's favorite. I assumed this was simple sisterly love and milked it for everything it was worth: guests would bring two presents on my brother's birthday because they knew I would start crying if I didn't get anything, too. My mother was constantly told to cover me up and say prayers for me so that I wouldn't get the evil eye (or as we say, *nazar na lag jaye*). This confused the hell out of me because such warnings were never given regarding my brother. Later I would understand that this was because I was fairer than him.

To fuss over skin color, especially the skin color of a child, is absurd. But it went even further. Before I went off to school, my beauty regimen (as prescribed by my mother) was to shower, get dressed, and apply a boatload of a "special cream" on my face so I didn't "catch the sun." I liked the smell, because it re-

*White girl.

minded me of my aunties, my older cousins, and even my mother. And if there's anything a little girl wants to be at the age of seven, it is to be like her mother. I felt like a real woman; someone who smelled faintly of roses and the same chemical that was apparently being injected into every moisturizer back home.

In 2014 I was introduced more specifically to the concept of colorism. At this point in my life, I had faced blatant and disgusting racism in high school for not being white, and was fetishized in adulthood for being "exotic," but I never discussed my color within the desi community. Then one day I witnessed a sudden uproar on Twitter from the African American community about the obvious bleaching and "whitewashing" of black bodies in the Western media. I became incredibly enraged that skin bleach was something being legally sold and regulated in communities of color.

Suddenly it all came back to me. The "special cream." The evil eye. Saloni. My brother. Eventually, the hashtag #UnfairAndLovely began to make its rounds online and I realized the rose-scented cream my mother applied on my face day and night was bleach. That bleach would ensure that their gori daughter stayed white so later in life she would have the privilege to be picked by a shadist asshole over someone darker.

In junior high, I was the last girl to start shaving her legs. To me, it wasn't such a big deal. Everyone has hair, right? I had stretch marks, bruises, and scars on my knees from climbing around exposed brick walls back home. I was chubby and had full lips. I sweat a LOT and had bushy brows and a thicker mustache than all the boys in my grade. I had features that were so very Indian, and I was often made to feel like they were alien or unnatural. Despite being born fair-skinned in my own culture, I felt an underlying pressure to become whiter. I truly believed that if I was whiter, I would be loved and appreciated more as a person. I knew that I was funny, talented, lovable, and much more on the inside, but my mind had convinced my eyes to see a face that just didn't communicate beauty. Everywhere I looked, I was overshadowed by a fairer body, who would almost always get the date, the grades, the job, the ring—everything.

It took me a long time to unlearn the teaching that lighter skin is more worthy of love than darker skin and that my Indian features were somehow less attractive, an idea that spans many cultures. It took even longer to reconcile the privilege of being lighter skinned within the desi community while facing racism outside it.

Fun fact: In addition to facial bleaching creams, companies across Asia market whitening/lightening creams for underarms and even the vagina. THE VAGINA. I'm packing my things and moving to Mars, because the world finds a new thing to hate about my body every year. Maybe out there I can be free to embrace all the dark corners of my body.

In the meantime, instead of supporting things like skin bleaching to fit a Eurocentric idea of beauty (I'm also looking at you, CONTOURING KITS), how about we develop beauty products that reflect our real selves like Broke 'n' Lovely or Short 'n' Lovely or Depressed Right Now but I'm Workin' on It 'n' Lovely. Dark 'n' Lovely.

IS THIS GORI WEARING A BINDI AGAIN?!
MMMHMM

BINDI: APPROPRIATE VS. APPROPRIATION

Dear non-desis: I get it. You love the way we look. We're colorful, radiant, shiny, and draped with luxurious silks and fabrics on a daily basis. It's easy to get caught up with the glamour of our culture because it's a culture of celebration. However, one must always remember that it is not YOUR culture of celebration. This means that you as a non-desi cannot simply use our culture to celebrate yourself. It doesn't mix, and it might offend. So to help you guys out, I've listed scenarios in which it is appropriate and most definitely INAPPROPRIATE to wear a bindi.

APPROPRIATE

When you are invited to an Indian, Pakistani, Bengali, Sri Lankan, Nepalese wedding.

~

When you are invited to any DESI event (desi = all of the above).

~

When you attend a religious ceremony.

~

If one of your parents is desi.

INAPPROPRIATE

Coachella.

~

In your bedroom, posing for an Instagram post.

~

At a "Beatles Go to India" themed birthday party.

~

For a Halloween party (our culture is NOT your costume).

HOW TO IGNORE BAKWAAS* CRITICISM
SAVE YOUR BAK BAK FOR SOMEONE WHO GIVES A FUCK FUCK.

*Nonsense.

"YOU'RE SO EXOTIC!"

When I was thirteen I happened to pass an older man who yelled, "Damn, you're an exotic beauty!" in my direction. To which I promptly yelled back, "I'm fucking thirteen, you perv!" Fetishizing people based on their race is racist. Deflect all bullshit disguised as compliments with swift force.

"YOU SHOULD LOSE SOME WEIGHT BEFORE THE WEDDING!"

Don't take this advice. Don't give this advice. Losing weight before a public event can be mentally and emotionally toxic, especially when it's not your own idea. You are beautiful and will remain that way regardless of how many aunties are there to tell you otherwise.

"WHEN WAS THE LAST TIME YOU WAXED?"

Reply with "Never!" And then run out the door, with the wind caressing your silky soft mustache strands. Facial hair is nothing to be embarrassed of. We all have it. It's natural. It's what makes us human. Don't be too hard on yourself about not ripping your sideburns off all the time; facial hair is a beautiful characteristic of our people and it looks adorable.

"YOU SHOULD MAKE FRIENDS WITH MORE OF OUR PEOPLE."

The most beautiful part about hanging out in the West is getting to know people from all over the world. Go out there and learn about everyone. We're all in this together, so we've got to make an effort to live in unison.

“YOU SHOULD STAY AT HOME AFTER HIGH SCHOOL AND LOOK FOR A HUSBAND.”

Why in the hell would you want to do that? Listen, keep your head in the books, get out there, and make something of yourself, kiddo. You’ve got one life and a ton of potential. Don’t worry about things like husbands—they will come into your world naturally, and exactly when you allow them to.

DOMES
SKILL
PAY
PART 5
ONE HUNDRED DOLLARS
100
HATECOPY!

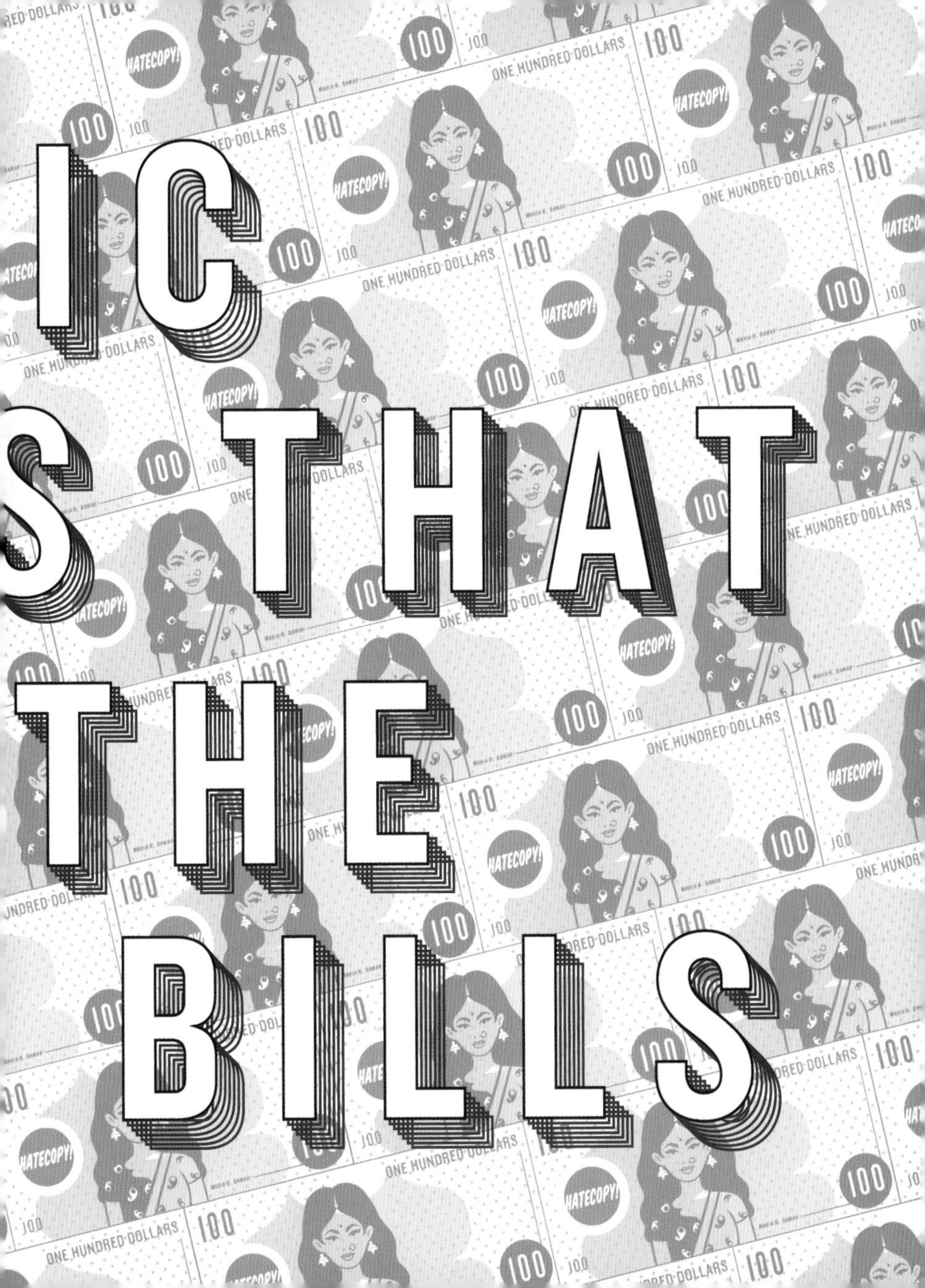
IC
S THAT
THE
BILLS
ONE HUNDRED DOLLARS
HATECOPY!
100

HOW TO DODGE A CHAPPAL
YOU WILL REMEMBER THIS BEATING FOR THE REST OF YOUR HARAMI LIFE!

You did it. You fucked up and got your mother so rattled that you now have to dodge her slipper, which is being hurled in your direction. Don't worry, I, too, have messed up enough in my lifetime to acquire a few insider tips and tricks to avoid getting blasted with a chappal. Watch and learn.

THE GEORGE W. BUSH

I couldn't write this chapter without mentioning the infamous GWB chappal dodge at least once. This method is best for dodging the airborne slipper. The technique is simple: Just move side to side and hope that you tire her out with your A-plus agility.

THE SPRINT

Follow your instincts and make a run for it. The key is to run into a public space screaming. This will distract slipper whippers so they have no choice but to act nice and save the whooping for another time. If you stay out long enough, they might forget.

Note: This will not work for all parents, and depends on how badly you messed up. There is still a slight chance that you might get your ass beat in public.

THE KUNG FU

When your legs have given up on you, it's time to get creative. The kung fu might not help you dodge the slipper, but it will definitely help you block them. Get your *Enter the Dragon* on and start deflecting the maternal wrath.

THE CHAMP

And when all else fails, your last resort is to sit there and take the chappal like a champ. This is a method that works to eliminate the slipper whipping altogether because it takes away the excitement of the chase. You will over time bore the whipper and force them to use different tactics that don't involve the chappal altogether. Success!

WTF IS "CURRY"?

I know, I know, you're probably like "Hatecopy, contrary to popular belief, there is no such dish in Indian culture called curry. Unless you are referring to the Gujarati/Rajasthani creamy and hearty dumpling stew called karhi, which is made with chickpea flour and yogurt. This is because our cuisine, although it may use curry leaves, does not actually require the ingredient called curry powder for any national dish. The term *curry* in most Western contexts simply refers to the hot spicy liquid that is not butter chicken served at every Indian restaurant."

And to that I say: You guys don't know what you're talking about. After arriving in the West I was thoroughly educated by my American and Canadian friends on what MY cuisine was actually called. I will now take this opportunity to pass this wisdom on to you so we can finally all start understanding and using the CORRECT terms for our food.

Traditional name:

ROGAN JOSH

Correct name:

CURRY

Context:

Rogan josh? Oh, I thought that was the name of your new boyfriend. Turns out it's just CURRY.

Traditional name:

CHICKEN KORMA/JALFREZI/ DOPIAZA

Correct name:

CHICKEN CURRY

Context:

Maria, I can't tell the difference between these three. They all look like CHICKEN CURRY to me.

Traditional name:

DAAL

Correct name:

LENTIL CURRY

Context:

Ew, why is it yellow? Oh, it's got LEGUMES. Must have a lot of fiber. I'll drink this out of a cup after yoga. Loving this LENTIL curry. Mmmmmm.

Traditional name:

NAAN

Correct name:

NAAN BREAD

Context:

Malini, this restaurant is one of my favorites. I come here all the time. The owners all love me. Hold up, let me order more NAAN BREAD for us.

Traditional name:

BIRYANI

Correct name:

OH, IT'S LIKE A RICE PILAF?!

Context:

What is this? Oh my god, it looks spicy. Does it have curry in it? OH, IT'S LIKE A RICE PILAF?!

Traditional name:

CHAI

Correct name:

CHAI TEA OR CHAI TEA LATTE FOR EXTRA REDUNDANCY

Context:

This place has the best chai tea latte.

Now that I have laid out some perfect examples, I hope that we can all ditch these ridiculous names for our dishes that clearly signify the region/history and ingredients involved. All you have to remember is that everything hot and saucy is a curry and everything else is "No thanks, I already ate."

SPICE METER

10 out of 10 green chilies. The guilt game is strong with this one. If you eat three rotis, yo can be damn sure there are three more comin your way.

CHARACTERISTICS

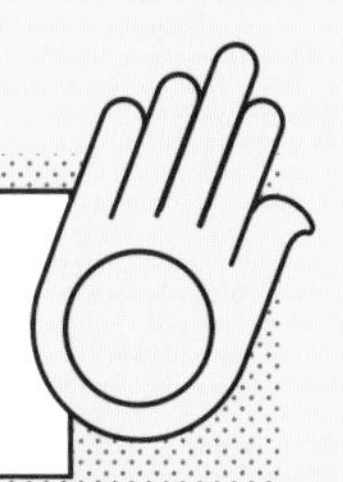

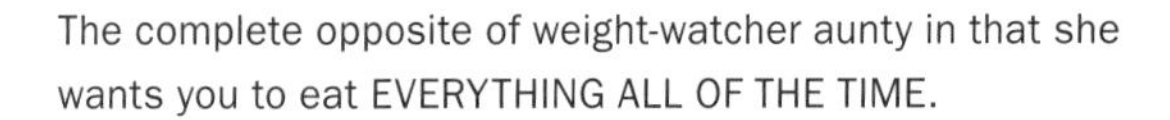

The complete opposite of weight-watcher aunty in that she wants you to eat EVERYTHING ALL OF THE TIME.

WHERE YOU MIGHT FIND THEM

Dinner parties, wedding buffets, dinner parties that are also buffets.

STRENGTHS

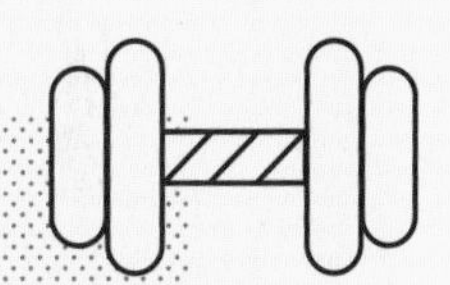

Finding ways to put more carbs on your plate.

WEAKNESSES

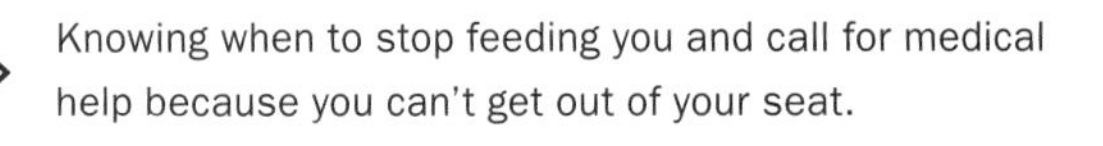

Knowing when to stop feeding you and call for medical help because you can't get out of your seat.

SCENARIO 1

YOU HAVE BEEN EATING FOR, LIKE, THIRTY MINUTES NOW. YOU'RE ON YOUR FIFTH ROTI AND YOU CAN'T EAT ANY MORE. YOU HAVE TO LET AUNTY KNOW WITHOUT GETTING RIDICULED.

Tell her you can't eat any more paneer because the paneer is starting to eat you from the inside.

Tell her you want to save space for the next time you see her. She doesn't hurl another roti in your direction, and you get to take a break from feeling like a human trash can.

HOW DARE YOU
INSULT MY COOKING?

When I was growing up, the only culinary advice my mother passed down to me was "get out of my kitchen," so naturally, I had to improvise and learn all these cool cooking and serving tips and tricks through trial and error and the Internet.

It's no secret that the desi diet includes so much grease and ghee that having high cholesterol has become sort of a rite of passage. You're not truly desi if you've never gotten the sweats from eating too much in one sitting. And unfortunately this was compromised when I was first introduced to the concept of "serving sizes." What?! The only serving size I know is putting enough on your plate so you didn't have to get up again to eat your thirds.

VEGETABLES

Nutritional:

HALF OF YOUR PLATE

Desi:

Sabji on TOP of the parantha. The plate is covered with the parantha. Slap on the butter a li'l bit. Oh, yeah, that's nice.

WHOLE GRAINS

Nutritional:

A FOURTH OF YOUR PLATE

Desi:

Biryani—all of the plate. Use raita to cover the fourth and mix it all up. Oh, God, yes.

PROTEIN

Nutritional:

A FOURTH OF YOUR PLATE

Desi:

Butter chicken dripping off the plate. Slap that shit on top of the rice and dunk your face in it like you're bobbing for apples. BREATHE IT IN. BE ONE WITH IT.

OIL

Nutritional:

HEALTHY PLANT OILS, SUCH AS OLIVE, SUNFLOWER, OR CANOLA OIL, BUT IN MODERATION

Desi:

If your food isn't swimming in oil, it's not worth eating. THROW IT OUT.

CHAI SHAI

Do you guys remember *The Princess Diaries*? I don't. But what I vaguely remember from the trailer is that Anne Hathaway basically had to go through the etiquette training that every desi girl has endured since birth. From cleaning the house to rolling a roti to serving chai.

Chai time is very important in a desi household. It is when friendships are made, bonds are built, marriages are arranged, and plans to destroy the sasural* are set. In our culture, one could say it's damn near criminal not to know how to make a good cup of chai. But then again, everyone is different, and how you make your chai says a lot about who you are.

THE SIDHA SADHA

This chai is made in the most harmless, basic way possible. A few tea bags, no sugar, enough to get everyone through the day.

THE MASALA MAMA

Oh, hot damn, what did you put IN THIS? This chai is extra enough to get a white person to invest in opening a franchise for you called Cinnamon & Co.

THE COLLEGE IDIOT

Harsh name for a harsh chai. It's 100 percent likely to have been made in the microwave with too much milk. Might as well have been a CHAI TEA LATTE.

THE CHAIWALA

This is the real deal. Whoever made this is either a chaiwala or an OG aunty straight from the motherland. This uses actual tea leaves, cardamom, whole milk, and love. Cherish it. Don't chug it.

*In-laws.

DON'T CRY OVER SPLIT CHAI

WHAT DOES YOUR ROTI SHAPE SAY ABOUT YOU?!

MATCH YOUR ROLLING SKILLS BELOW AND FIND OUT JUST HOW DISAPPOINTED YOUR IN-LAWS WIL BE!!!

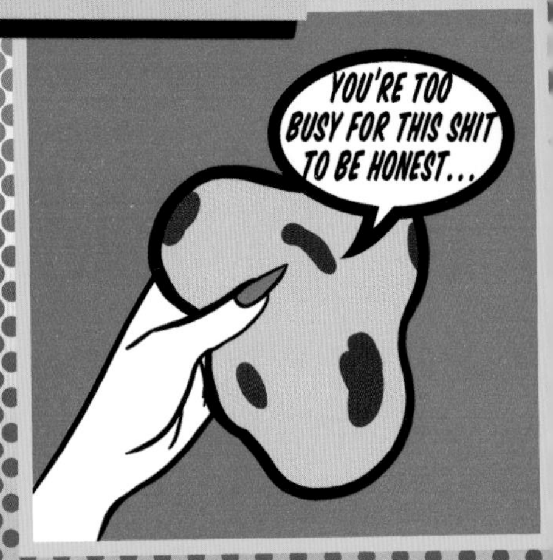

WHAT YOUR ROTI SHAPE SAYS ABOUT YOU

We have all been in the kitchen at one point faced with the challenge of rolling a perfectly round roti. A lot of us took this challenge and sucked at it. But somehow competitiveness and determination got the best of us and we ended up practicing until we kinda sorta got it right. But no two rotis are alike, and how you roll one is a big indicator of how you've been getting by this whole time.

Match your rolling skills and find out just how disappointed your in-laws will be!

PART 6
LIFE,
STYLE

LIFE-
STYLE

HOW TO WRAP A SAREE

You've got your hair and makeup done and now it's time to put on the saree. The only thing is, all the aunties have left already and you're stuck with your best friend and your EXTREMELY talkative seven-year-old niece. You've got two options. The first is to yell out instructions from Google while your BFFL and niece scramble to follow them, which eventually leads to your BFFL stabbing your niece with a pin and now there's blood on the petticoat and a very, very angry little girl trying to dial 911.

OR

Follow these helpful tips below.

WEAR THE BLOUSE. BUTTONS GO IN THE FRONT, NOT THE BACK.

I made this mistake once. If you're wearing the blouse (which is the little crop top) and it has buttons, they gotta go where the boobs are. The back of the blouse should be the lower part, with the strings tied into a sexy little bow.

PUT ON THE PETTICOAT.

Petticoat is just an old-timey way to say underskirt. This is the thin layer of fabric that keeps the rest of the saree up. Typically, older models of the petticoat have a drawstring that you have to tie up REAAAALLLY tight, just below the belly button. It will make a little bit of muffin top, but, hey, that's some old Bollywood sexiness right there. And don't worry, the extra fabric from the saree will balance it out.

STEP 3

IT'S TIME TO WRAP IT UP.

There are two ends to the miles and miles of saree fabric; one end is more heavily embroidered than the other. The less embroidered end must be wrapped and tucked in the petticoat first. Pin it in if you must. That first roll around your waist will set the length and tightness of your saree, so make sure it's to your liking.

STEP 4

CREATE THE PLEATS.

This is the little wavy part in the front of the saree that gives you that sexy mermaid effect. Zigzag your extra fabric after rolling it around a few times to create that harmonica look. Take all the folds you've created together, shuffle them to even them out, and pin them together with a large safety pin. You can then take the cluster of folds and tuck them into the petticoat with the rest of the saree. PIN THAT SHIT IN PLACE.

STEP 5

THROW THE MORE HEAVILY EMBROIDERED END OF THE FABRIC OVER YOUR SHOULDER.

Take your other hand and bring the extra fabric around the back for an elegant look. I just fold the extra fabric over one shoulder and pin it to the blouse so I can dance without having to fuss with it all night.

And that is all! You've done it. It takes a little practice, but the key is to PIN, PIN, PIN it until it looks right. The good thing about a saree is that it's all basically freestyle and morphs to your body, so it's very hard to mess up if all you're doing is wrapping it around your own curves. You're gonna do great, beti. I believe in you. **GOOD LUCK.**

THE ONLINE STALKER AUNTY
I'M HERE TO DRINK CHAI AND LURK FACEBOOK..
SPICE RATING?
9/10
SPICE METER

9 out of 10 green chilies. Aside from capturing each and every second of your existence and posting it in her online photo albums, the OS aunty can be a risk to befriend online. Especially if you plan to upload pics in your teeny-weeny Hello Kitty bikini this summer.

CHARACTERISTICS

The online stalker aunty is a tech-savvy lady who has enough time to follow each and every one of your relatives on social media.

WHERE YOU MIGHT FIND THEM

Much like Planet Earth, the Internet can be a small space. You won't need to look far to find her, because chances are she's found you first.

STRENGTHS

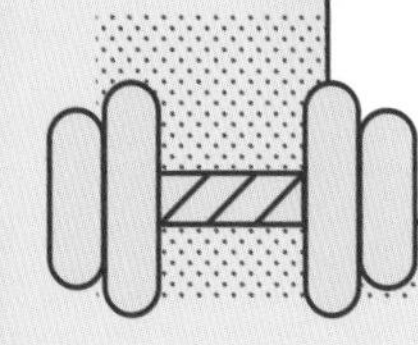

Uploading unflattering photos of you stuffing your face at cousin Pinky's baby shower.

WEAKNESSES

Lucky for you, the OS aunty doesn't know how to take a screenshot. So if you do have photos of yourself getting absolutely annihilated at the local bar with your Tinder date last night, DELETE THEM BEFORE SHE FINDS OUT.

SCENARIO 1

YOU JUST BEFRIENDED OS AUNTY AND SHE HAS COMMENTED ON YOUR PIC FROM HALLOWEEN. YOU WERE DRESSED AS A SEXY COP.

ROOKIE MOVE

Tell her you were training to protect the neighborhood and were caught in a high-speed chase when your boobs fell out.

BOSS MOVE

Tell her you have a skimpier saree that you plan to wear at the next dinner party.

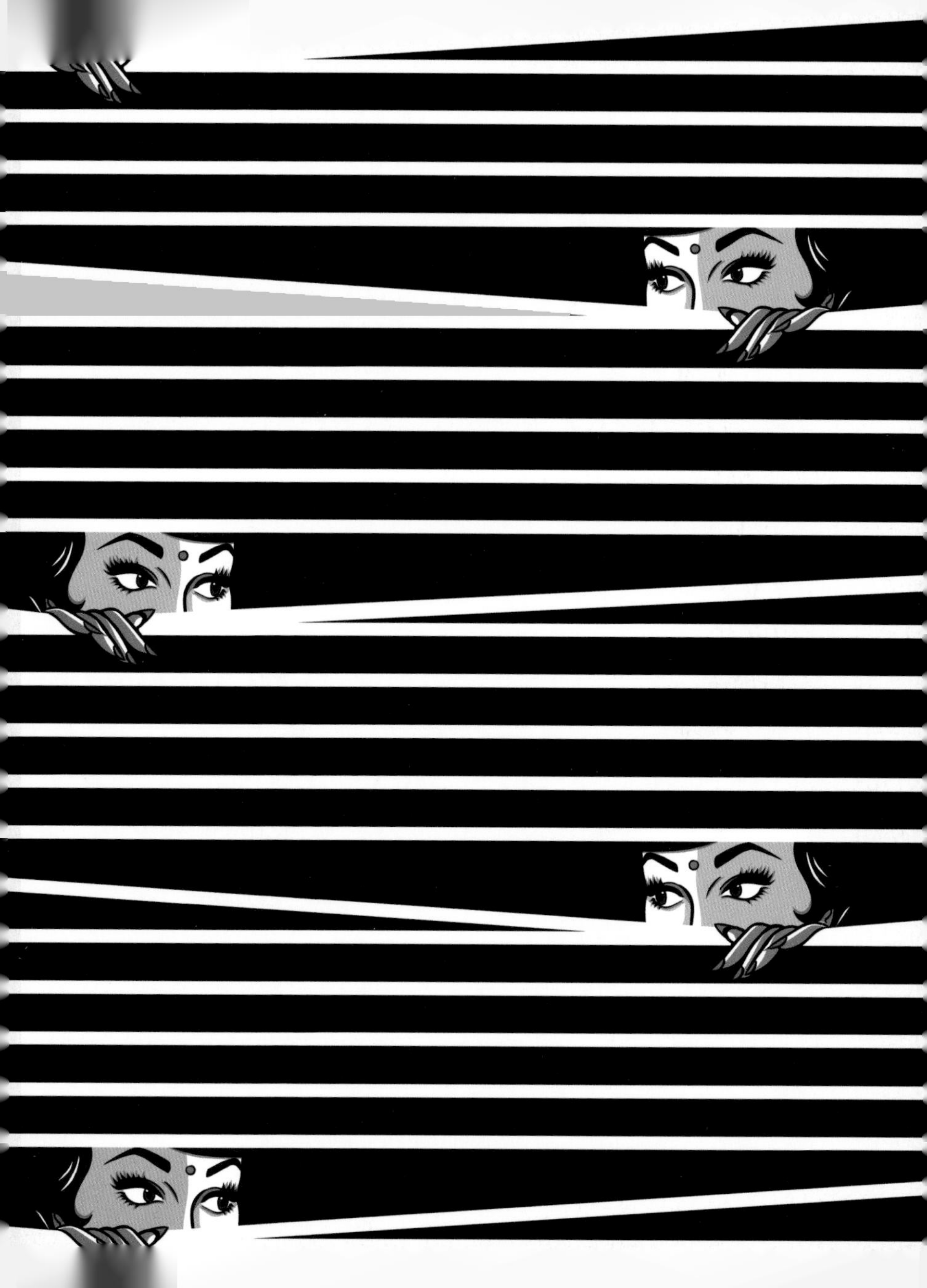

SPICE METER

10 out of 10 green chilies. She was made for the limelight. She must be the life of every party wit her super-choreographed hip thrusts and manic twirls. She will laugh the loudest and cry the hardest. Invite her to the next wedding or funera She'll really get everyone going.

CHARACTERISTICS

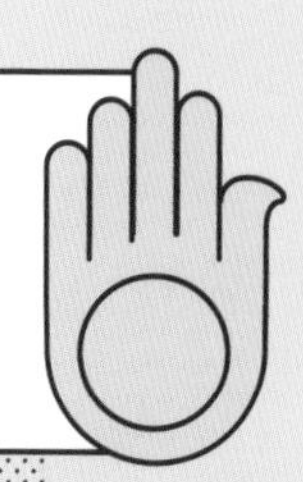

If hyperbole was a person, the Bollywood aunty would be it. She has learned all of her mannerisms and dialogues from pop culture. Anything and everything will be blown out of proportion, so don't take it to heart.

WHERE YOU MIGHT FIND THEM

Aside from Yash Raj films, you can find the Bollywood aunty faintly crying in the distance every time you do something a good girl shouldn't.

STRENGTHS

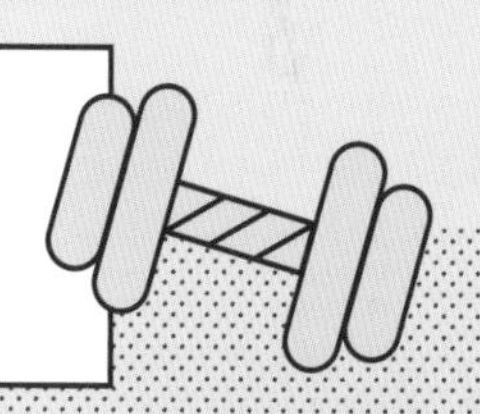

Crying over everything. Dropping to the ground, beating her chest, and yelling, "I'M RUINED!! WE ARE ALL RUINED!!"

WEAKNESSES

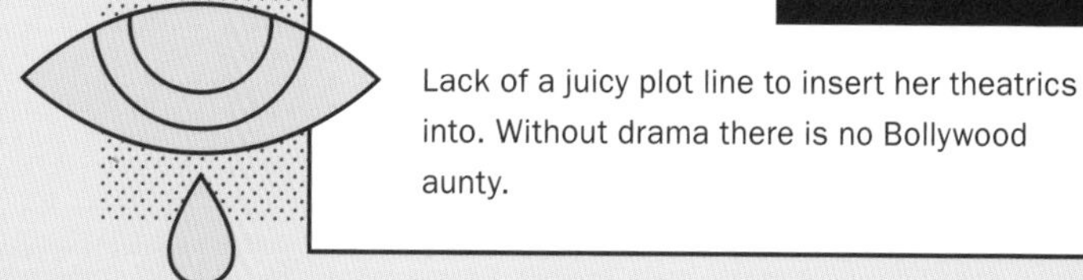

Lack of a juicy plot line to insert her theatrics into. Without drama there is no Bollywood aunty.

SCENARIO 1

YOU HAVE DECIDED TO TAKE A FEW SHOTS OF TEQUILA BEFORE HITTING THE DANCE FLOOR AT YOUR BEST FRIEND'S WEDDING. BOLLYWOOD AUNTY CAUGHT YOU. YOU ARE NOW GETTING THE DEATH STARE. SHE ADMONISHES YOU: "NICE GIRLS DON'T DO DARU [THE AFOREMENTIONED LIQUOR]!"

ROOKIE MOVE

Tell her you are holding it for one of the boys. You have never touched alcohol in your life and swear that a nice cold glass of lassi made from the freshest 100 percent goat's milk will give you MORE energy.

BOSS MOVE

Maintain eye contact while taking the shot. Offer her one.

NICE GIRLS DON'T DO DARU!

SCENARIO II

BOLLYWOOD AUNTY'S HUSBAND DECIDED TO LEAVE HER. SHE SUSPECTS THAT HE WAS HAVING AN EXTRAMARITAL AFFAIR WITH SOMEONE SHE KNOWS.

ROOKIE MOVE

Comfort her and tell her that it was for the best and that eventually she will move on.

BOSS MOVE

Tell her the affair was with your mom. Entertainment for DAYS.

SIMRAN, STAY AWAY
ROM MY HUSBAND!

THE ANONYMOUS AUNTY

I'LL STEP ON HER SAREE.

SPICE RATING?

7/10

SPICE METER

7 out of 10 green chilies. Nothing against you personally. Her favorite drama series is off the air, so anonymous aunty is just here to watch some real-life drama unfold.

CHARACTERISTICS

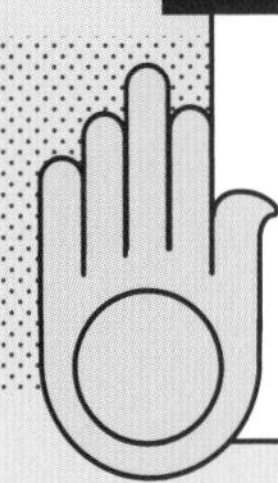

No, anonymous aunty is not a part of a secret underground Internet hacker group that plots to bring justice into the world, but she's pretty close! She's the plus-one aunty that shows up to every gathering, adding the tiebreaker vote in conversations that have nothing to do with her.

WHERE YOU MIGHT FIND THEM

You can find anonymous aunty in situations where a third opinion is needed to settle the matter. She could be the aunty your mother calls up to get advice on how to keep you from embarrassing the family again. She could be that little voice that chimes in with "Listen to our advice seriously, beta," in an argument between you and your mother. How or when she arrived at your house to say this, you will never know.

STRENGTHS

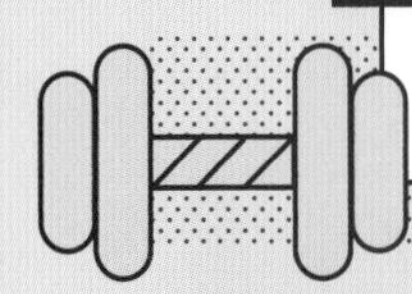

Being the yes-man to all the naysayers.

WEAKNESSES

Taking your side.

SCENARIO 1

YOU ARE BEING ROASTED BY A GROUP OF AUNTIES FOR SOMETHING SMALL. ANONYMOUS AUNTY APPEARS OUT OF NOWHERE TO ADD HER TWO CENTS.

Acknowledge her presence and laugh nervously until everyone realizes you're a helpless target. Pray that they move on to grilling someone else.

Make up some wild dramatic statement to get anonymous aunty to admit to something. "Hey, didn't you say the same thing about [aunty standing next to you]?"

HAS ANYONE SEEN MY BIWI? SHE'S THE ONE TALKING SHIT.

SCENARIO II

AA HAS DECIDED TO BACK YOUR MOTHER UP ON HER CLAIM THAT YOU SHOULD DEFINITELY CREATE AN ONLINE ACCOUNT ON A MATRIMONY WEBSITE.

ROOKIE MOVE

There is strength in numbers, so your mother and this random aunty must be right if they BOTH agree on this one wild idea. It's your life, after all. Why not leave it in the hands of some lady who saw you once when you were five?

BOSS MOVE

Create that matrimony account under AA's name (or the name you decided to give her; Kaanta Ben sounds pretty legit).

I MET YOUR LOSER UNCLE THIS WAY. TRUST ME! IT WORKS!

THINGS THAT SHOULD EXIST IN DESI CULTURE BUT DON'T

MINI ROTI

There is not a single day that goes by when I don't think about tandoori tacos made with miniature rotis. If only there was a trend of eating little rotis on the go instead of one giant flour blanket during mealtime. PORTION CONTROL, PEOPLE!

SNAP-ON SAREE

It's been five days and you're still trying to figure out how to fold all this fabric without playing cat's cradle with your limbs. Why not have a saree that you can snap on and tear off at any given time? I'm so sure there has to be something like this out there. But if there isn't, CAN WE GET ON IT?

SPICE GUN

We have a zillion spices. We should shoot them all into the pot with a spice gun. It can make little Bollywood gun sounds as you shoot it. You can even use it for self-defense!

DISCLAIMER FOR A BOLLYWOOD FLICK THAT LETS YOU KNOW IF IT IS ACTUALLY AN ADAPTATION OF AN OLD ENGLISH FILM

There have been countless times when I would be watching a movie and wondering who in the hell would green-light such an unrealistic idea. Only to find out a google later that the plot line would have made more sense had I watched the original IRISH version of the story from 1983.

KUTTA KURTA

Okay, how adorable is this idea? I've never seen pets at an Indian wedding, but that's probably because they didn't have anything fancy to wear! Kutta kurtas are a great way to dress up your fluffy best friends and have them be a part of the fun. Sabyasachi, take notes.

FREE HENNA IDEAS FOR YOUR NEXT WEDDING

MAP OF THE WEDDING HALL

You can get your henna artist to draw a map of the venue so you know all of the possible exits to dodge aunties with. It will also help you plan out the fastest route to the buffet.

SECRET SEXY MESSAGES

This one is my personal favorite. Write down hot little messages (or even your phone number) across both palms, then flash them to the hot guy across the hall. His mother will never find out.

YOUR TO-DO LIST FOR THE WEEK

Listen, this stuff doesn't wash off for at least a week. Take advantage of that and list everything from doing your laundry to taking the dog to the vet. It's paperless, organic, and totally game-changing.

A GIANT NO

"Are you married yet?" "Did you get a job?" "Are you on a diet?" "Are your parents taking you back to India?" You're going to be using this a lot in conversation, so give your vocal cords a break and use your hands instead.

NAMES OF EVERYONE WHO CUT IN FRONT OF YOU AT THE BUFFET

Never forget your enemies. Never let them forget you.

ALL OF YOUR PASSWORDS

This isn't exactly practical, but it's very helpful if you keep forgetting them. Maybe throw in a fake password to throw a hacker off.

AN OUTLINE OF ALL THE COOL PERMANENT TATTOOS YOU'VE ALWAYS WANTED BUT WILL GET YOUR ASS BEAT IF YOU GO THROUGH WITH THEM

That cool knuckle tat that reads RUDE BETI? You can go ahead and get it. It'll wash off in a week.

WHAT WOULD SOCIETY SAY?!

WHAT WOULD SOCIETY THINK?

For as long as I can remember, I've heard my mother and my aunties scream the phrase "LOG KYA KAHENGE?!" which translates to "What will people SAY?!" This phrase normally follows when one of the kids did anything outside the cultural norm, like joining a sports team while having a vagina or taking up singing while not having a vagina. Every lifestyle decision was measured against what opinions our neighbors would have on the matter.

This attitude didn't just affect the kids. Within our family, discussing bigger issues like divorce and mental illness were avoided in order to escape the criticism of strangers. Everyone was so hush-hush about things outside the "norm" that life became a distorted version of keeping up with the Joneses, and the facade immediately fell apart as soon as we entered college.

Looking back at all the conversations we avoided with our families out of fear of being judged, I've made this section to confront the truths of what would have actually happened if we were open about ourselves.

"MOM, DAD, I HAVE A BOYFRIEND."

What they think society would say: SHE IS RUNNING AROUND WITH BOYS! WHO WILL MARRY HER?!

What society would actually say: You go, girl. He's got a great face. Just stop making out at the PlayPlace in the local McDonald's.

"MOM, DAD, I DON'T WANT TO GO TO UNIVERSITY. I WANT TO BECOME A RAPPER."

What they think society would say: THEY HAVE THROWN THEIR LIFE AWAY! THEIR KIDS ARE SPOILED!

What society would actually say: That mixtape better be fire.

"MOM, DAD, I WANT TO MOVE OUT."

What they think society would say: WHAT?! MOVING OUT WITHOUT MARRIAGE? WHO DO THEY THINK THEY ARE?! THESE CHILDREN DON'T LOVE THEIR FAMILY!

What society would actually say: Your water bill is overdue. Stop spending so much on margaritas.

All in all, we've got to stop worrying so much about what others think of our families and focus on talking more with one another. We would have a much easier time getting along and tackling real issues like homophobia, racism, and sexism within our communities if parents and children talk openly. We come from a beautiful, liberal, and colorful culture; hell, we're the ones who created the Kama Sutra. We've been rooted in thinking outside the box for as long as we've been around. It's only fair that we continue breaking barriers and end stigmatizing lifestyles that are different.

Good luck!

BUT WHY AUNTIES?!

Because my mother knows so many aunties, I asked her to talk about what it means to be an aunty and to share some insight into the minds of women who dish out unsolicited advice like it's Halloween candy.

Me: Mom, why do you think aunties give out so much advice for no reason?

Mom: Firstly, Maria, don't write anything stupid about me in your book, because I will deny everything.

Me: Okay. Answer the question, please.

Mom: Aunties say these things because they like to feel like they are watching over you, as if you were their own daughter or son.

Me: Even when you're not related to them.

Mom: It is up to you to take the advice. If you think it will benefit you, then good. If not, then you can ignore it.

Me: So we should ignore the aunties?

Mom: If you don't think the advice applies. We want to guide our children to be better people and to teach you our values.

Me: But most of the "children" receiving this advice are adults. Some are young adults. A lot of the advice has to do with marriage.

Mom: You must always respect your elders.

Me: Yes, but—

Mom: See, I should have taught you more values. You must listen to your parents. AND NOT YELL AT THEM!

Me: This is going off topic—

Mom: Listen, when we brought you here, we had no idea you guys would be so adaptive and learn so much from other cultures. We didn't know what we were dealing with. All we can do is remind you to respect your elders and know who you really are.

Me: Should elders be expected to respect us back?

Mom: Your elders will respect you when you listen to them.

Me: Good loophole.

Our conversation went in a few circles before landing on the conclusion that aunties will be aunties and uncles will be uncles. Our culture is so deeply rooted in family values that nothing will change that. Our dramas will continue to be livelier, our food will be spicier, our advice will be uncalled for, and our homes will be powered by the constant playful sass between young people and their elders. This is a dynamic as old as our culture itself, and it will be funny to see what happens when we attempt to pass our own advice down to the generations to come. Maybe there will be a sequel written by an even louder kutti (or kutta) than me. And who knows what kind of things we will get called out for? Nagging them to stop playing with their weird AI robot best friends and make some real ones? Insisting that they eat actual food instead of taking supplement pills?

"Travel to our dimension for dinner sometime, you ungrateful child!! YOUR FATHER AND I FORGOT WHAT YOUR PHYSICAL FORM LOOKS LIKE! AND CLEAN UP YOUR HARD DRIVE. IT'S A GODDAMN MESS!"

It's only a matter of time.

FUCK, I'M AN AUNTY!

1 out of 10 green chilies. Not spicy, just exhausting. The best way to deal with an unclesplainer is to report his behavior to your mother. Who will then report to his wife. Who will then add extra spice to his korma as punishment.

CHARACTERISTICS

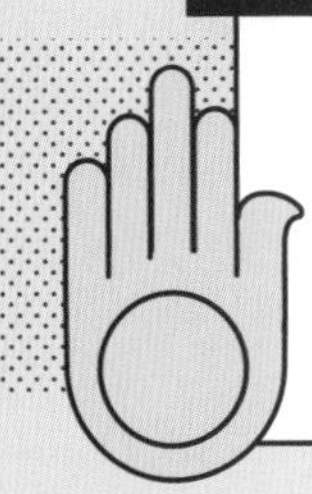

Did you ever watch *The Wizard of Oz* without getting bored? I did once. And the unclesplainer is kind of like the Wizard: dispensing unsolicited advice behind the curtain. He is a mansplainer and aunty whisperer in one.

WHERE YOU MIGHT FIND THEM

Hiding behind an aunty.

STRENGTHS

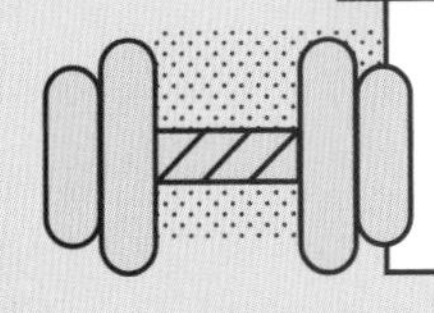

Coming up with new ways to keep people with vaginas from doing things "girls shouldn't do."

WEAKNESSES

Non-male opinions.

ACKNOWLEDGMENTS

WOW, GOOD JOB, BETA—YOU'VE REACHED THE END OF THE BOOK. I'M IMPRESSED. EVEN I HAVEN'T REACHED THIS FAR IN ONE GO AND I WROTE THIS SHIT. ANYWAY, THIS IS THE PART WHERE I THANK A BUNCH OF PEOPLE WHO ARE VERY NEAR AND DEAR TO MY LIFE. YOU CAN GOOGLE THEM OR WHATEVER IF YOU CARE ENOUGH, AND I CAN ASSURE YOU THEY'RE FAR MORE INTERESTING THAN ME. AFTER ALL, WITHOUT THE INFLUENCES AND PERSONALITIES OF THESE LOVELY PEOPLE, I WOULDN'T BE THE BAD BETI THAT I AM TODAY.

MAA

My mother used to visit the YWCA. They gave her clothes and prepared her for the one job interview she landed a few weeks after we moved to Canada. They taught her how to build a résumé, how to introduce herself, and how to pronounce certain English phrases correctly. When she eventually landed the job (which, of course, she did—she's literally a *genius*), she had to travel approximately two hours by train to go there. She saved every penny to provide for her family and never made us feel like anything was missing in our lives, even though most days we had enough to barely get by. And she did this while being my mother. Can you imagine? Sorry, Maa, for being such a royal pain in the ass but also thank you for not disowning me even though you threatened to do so, like, five thousand times. I'm grateful for your bravery, your resilience, your patience, and your wisdom. I couldn't have wished for a better, funnier, and feistier role model than you. You're a survivor and definitely the coolest aunty I know.

BRO

This section's for my brother. He's my hero, my rival, and the only person I have ever drop-kicked (*by accident*). Ever since I was born I've wanted to be just like him. I wanted to dress like him, talk like him, and be good at everything just like he is. If any aunty needed that all-around good guy to compare your dumbass to, my brother was that guy. And he still is. This guy has never made a bad decision in his life, I swear to God. Everyone loves him and it's infuriating but also kinda bragworthy. I'm sure life wasn't so easy for him either—after all, we grew up together—but you would never be able to tell. And that's the kind of grace I hope to possess someday. He encouraged me to rebel, to get out of the house, and see the world for myself, and it was the best advice I have ever got in my life. Period.

DAD

Thank you for being patient with me. I'm sorry for that chapter about the dude in the closet.

KAREN & CRESS

I would also like to thank the woman who gave me my first-ever job, Karen Howe, for the opportunity, the strength, and the courage to eventually become my own boss. Karen taught me a lot about standing up for myself in the male-dominated world of business, and seeing her break down patriarchal barriers inspired me to do so as well. Alongside her, my best friend, art director and teacher Cressida Sobrevilla, for being a part of my life and allowing me to observe quietly late at night in our ad agency office as she tinkered with Photoshop to bring our ideas to life. Because of you, I had the courage to start over and pursue the arts.

BABBU

After getting laid off, I made a friend on the Internet. She was this tiny bombshell who had my exact same haircut and made me go, "Damn, we should be friends." That friend ended up being the girl I shared three exhibits and a Euro trip with and her name is Babneet Lakhesar. Babbu, as we lovingly call her, was my first true source of encouragement, the first person to truly believe in my work. She understood and shared my vision and, most important, showed me how to believe in myself. She possesses the strength and courage of a lioness and inspires me to fight for what I believe in, even when she's oceans away. She is a fighter, a visionary, and the kind of person that'll call you out on your bullshit the second she meets you. Everyone should be more like Babbu.

MONIKA & LAUREN

I still remember the feeling I had when I read Monika's e-mail signature, frantically trying to google the name of her agency and figuring out if this was all a prank. Luckily, she's legit and it wasn't a prank. I would like to thank Monika Verma and Lauren Spiegel for believing in my work and providing me with the opportunity to create this book. I would also like to thank them both for listening to my rants about breakups and various medical emergencies and more breakups. These two women have been my heroes and have cheered me up during times when the only words that would make me forget about my shitty life were, "Maria, you're writing a book!" Thank you so much for the opportunity and for the journey we will continue on together. I can't wait.

BADBOIRICHI

Every creative needs a skillful art director to thrive, and no one understands this better than Richard Dao. Without this guy, you would have been reading a bunch of pages thrown together like a bad third grade art project. A gazillion thank-yous to Richard for being a part of this project and for beautifully executing the book we are holding today. He's a lifesaver.

MINDY

I remember when *The Mindy Project* first aired. I actually heard about it from my brother and began watching it with him whenever we both visited our parents. It was one of those moments when we realized we may have a third sibling, and she played a sassy ob-gyn on TV. Mindy Kaling was one of those women I felt instantly connected to, not only because of her work but because of her hustle. My brother and I had been fans of her since *The Office*, so you can imagine the screaming and crying when we found out she's a fan of my work as well. I'm still over the moon and thankful for her support and for allowing me to share my work with her. She is an endless source of motivation and someone I will always look up to as my personal hero.

AND, OF COURSE

All my actual aunties back home and around the world

Tova Hasiwar
Sarah Chaudry
Robert McRae
the Lakhesar family
Nuvango
Gaurav Sawhney
Mriga & Amrit
Samira Maharaj
Zachary Roher
Alex Boyman
Elle Canada
Manisha Claire
Kajal Mag
Raju

1950 Collective
Choti Maria
Scaachi Koul
Atif & Humai (HYFN)

and everyone who has supported my work by coming to my exhibits, sharing my art, and buying my little trinkets. Thank you for giving me the confidence to believe in myself and to live a life I thought was just a dream.

ABOUT THE AUTHOR

Maria Qamar, otherwise known as Hatecopy (@Hatecopy), is an artist living in Toronto. She was raised a first-generation Canadian in a traditional South Asian home. Maria worked in advertising before she started illustrating and posting her hilarious insights into diaspora culture and the significance of aunties in Indian culture to her Instagram account in February 2015. *Trust No Aunty* is her first book.